THE BIBLE STUDY

YOUTH EDITION

A 90-DAY STUDY OF THE BIBLE AND HOW IT RELATES TO YOU

D1441558

ZACH WINDAHL

ISBN 978-0-9984910-2-8

For Worldwide Distribution

Printed in China

Words by Zach Windahl

Design by Zach Windahl and Katlyn Hovland

Web: www.thebrandsunday.com

Email: zach@thebrandsunday.com

Instagram: @zachwindahl

TO THE BIBLE STUDY

WELCOME

YOUTH EDITION

INTRODUCTION

I know that god aligned our paths on purpose, and I couldn't be more excited about what he is going to do in your life during this 90-day journey together through the bible. By the time we are finished, you will have read the entire new testament and gone through overviews from each book of the old testament.

My prayer is not only for you to have a better understanding of the word, but that you will also find a better sense of meaning for your life and really understand the heart of our father. He loves you so much. It's amazing.

Before we dive in, I want to share a little bit about my testimony. Who knows, you and I might even share some things in common. We're in this thing called life together. Let's go!

My search for meaning

Identity.

It's what makes you…you.

For many of us it takes years to figure out who we are and what we want to be. For some it comes easy, for others it takes a lifetime.

We have society, parents, teachers, friends, siblings, girlfriends, boyfriends, all telling us how we should be. Everybody in your life has an idea of how you should live and act.

Why is it so easy for them to see it, but so difficult for us to figure out?

If you're like me, I spent years trying to be the person that everyone else wanted me to be. Growing up, people would constantly tell me that I was going to be famous some day and that I should do this or that with my life. It all came from the fact that I was an entrepreneur from an early age and had a pretty unhealthy work ethic to back it. But it didn't matter how unhealthy that work ethic was because I was going to be famous some day and be seen with the elite lol. Or at least that's what I was told.

So my head grew.

And grew. And grew.

And grew.

I believed the hype and did all that I could to live it.

You see, I'm a product of my society. I'm a Bachelor's Degree graduate with $70k in debt from a Christian University that did anything but spark my interest in God, it actually pushed me farther away. Little did I know that the darkness inside of me at the time didn't like the Light inside of the students. Funny how that happens. So, after graduating, I had quite a bad taste in my mouth.

But, I kept talking the talk. I wrote two Christian books my senior year, but didn't have the nerve to promote them like I should have since I didn't even believe what was coming out of my mouth. I went on to run a clothing line and recording with some friends, which I left after a few years. I worked on some other entrepreneurial projects after that, but the hard work that I was putting into them was not lining up with the success (or lack thereof). Everything that I touched began to fail. I was "good" though. Or at least that's what I told myself.

In reality, I had no direction for where to go from there. I remember sitting in my car outside of Starbucks talking to my friend Geoff about it. I had never felt so lost in my life. If you know me, you know I always have a plan. But this time I didn't. I was at the bottom. Broken and lost. I had spend the last several years focusing on myself and trying to become the best person I could be. But, to tell you the truth, I'm weak when I try to live life on my own. From the outside, everything looked great but the inside was a whole different story. Even though I thought I was "the man", I was still lacking something. My pride was fully intact, but my heart desired more.

I started to contemplate what all of this was about. I grew up considering myself a Christian, but I had no idea what that truly meant. I hadn't been following God's call at all. I still believed in Him, I just wasn't pursuing Him. I hadn't been to church in over a year for the simple fact that I couldn't stand the majority of Christians that I met because I didn't trust them. They all seemed so fake. So I sat there thinking…

Is life really all about going to college, getting a job, getting married, having kids, buying new things, and then (hopefully) one day retiring so I can enjoy life?

Really? That's it? That all seemed so shallow to me.

Then, let's look at religion. Every religion outside of Christianity takes their faith so seriously, it's insane. And then there's us. Where only 30% of Christians even read the Bible and the fact that a ton of "Christian" ideals are pretty skewed from the Bible itself - I was fed up.

So I read the Bible. Front to back. In 90 days.

I was blown away by how different the Bible actually is, compared to how it's presented in America. But that's what makes us Christians, right? The fact that we believe and follow Jesus?

Nothing was lining up. I was confused.

So I went on my own "Search for Meaning" journey. I quit my job and moved to a little beach town on the Sunshine Coast of Australia for 9 months to study the Bible for twelve hours a day, six days a week. That's a pretty big leap if you ask me. And at 27 years old it may not have been the wisest of decisions, but I wouldn't have changed it for anything.

My whole reason for this journey was to build a firm foundation in my faith - one that could not be crumbled by society. And that's exactly what I got, plus more.

And that's what my hope is for you - that you are able to build a firm foundation in your faith over the next year. Especially in a time when understanding the Word is one of the most important things that you can do.

GOALS

It doesn't matter what you have done in the past. What matters is now. God loves you SO much and is SO delighted that you want to spend time getting to know Him through Scripture.

Where are you currently at in your faith journey?
List 3 things that you want to get out of this study.

_____

_____

_____

_____

_____

_____

_____

_____

_____

_____

_____

_____

_____

NEW TESTAMENT

FACTS

Gospels

Matthew
Mark
Luke
John

Acts

Acts

Pauline
Epistles

Romans
1 Corinthians
2 Corinthians
Galasians
Ephesians
Phillipians
Colossians
1 Thessalonians
2 Thessalonians
1 Timothy
2 Timothy
Titus
Philemon

Hebrew
Christian
Epistles

Hebrews
James
1 Peter
2 Peter
1 John
2 John
3 John
Jude

Revelation

Revelation

27 Books
Greek language
First century AD

Key Characters

JOHN THE BAPTIST:

John the Baptist, was the final prophet of the Old Testament who arose after the 400 years of silence that followed the words of Malachi. He was the forerunner of Christ that was to pave the way and prepare the people for Jesus' arrival.

DISCIPLES:

The word "disciple" means, "a follower or student of a teacher, leader, or philosopher" (oxforddictionaries.com). When we talk about the disciples of Jesus, we refer to his twelve closest friends while on Earth. They were Andrew, Bartholomew, James son of Zebedee, James son of Alphaeus, John, Judas Iscariot, Jude the brother of James, Matthew, Peter, Philip, Simon the Zealot, and Thomas. One thing to note is that the majority of disciples were teenagers - how cool is that?!

JOHN:

John was known as the "Beloved Disciple" because of how much Jesus loved him. He was faithful until the end and was entrusted with taking care of Mary, the mother of Jesus. He wrote one of the Gospels, three letters to his churches in Asia Minor, and the book of Revelation.

JESUS:

God in the flesh. No need to explain. Read his words and have your mind blown.

PAUL:

Paul was known as the Hebrew of Hebrews, having studied under the great Gamaliel and was an extreme Pharisee by nature. Paul experience a radical conversion to Christ (which we will read about in the book of Acts), and he became the greatest missionary of the early Church. Paul founded many churches around the Greco-Roman world, and today we have letters to some of those churches that give us the groundwork for our theology.

LUKE:

Luke was a physician that partnered with Paul during a portion of his missionary work. He was also the author of a Gospel and the book of Acts, which were both used as testimonies in Paul's Roman trial.

PETER:

Peter was the first disciple that Jesus called to follow him. Jesus knew that he would be a great voice for the Kingdom so he changed his name from Simon (meaning "reed") to Peter (meaning "rock") and claimed that the Church would be built upon him. Peter had his ups and downs, but remained faithful to the end. He also gave us some amazing words recorded in his sermon on the day of Pentecost and in his two follow-up epistles.

PETER:

Timothy was Paul's spiritual son and was greatly loved by Paul himself. He also helped write a few of Paul's letters and had two letters written to him by Paul as encouragement to stand strong in the faith and continue on with the gospel message.

JAMES:

James was a brother of Jesus that didn't believe Jesus was the Messiah until after his resurrection. James, then became one of the top leaders for the church in Jerusalem and was highly respected among other believers. He ended up writing the book of James as "wisdom literature" to be added to the New Testament. It has been told that after he was martyred, his friends saw his knees for the first time and they were like the knees of camels from spending so much time in prayer.

READ: Mark 1-5

AUTHOR: Mark aka John Mark

DATE: AD 55-60 or AD 64-68

AUDIENCE: Christians in Rome

THEME: Jesus as the suffering servant

DAY ONE

OVERVIEW:

Mark is a unique book, in that it highlights miracles far more than teachings. He includes 18 miracles in these 16 chapters, with only four parables and one major discourse. Mark does not give any of Christ's ancestry, since the theme is that Christ is a servant, and people don't care about a servant's ancestry.

Mark himself was too young to be a disciple, but he was fascinated with Jesus so he hung around him as much as possible. He was also hyperactive. The word "immediately" is repeated 41x because he was always on the go from one place to the next. He couldn't sit still and wanted to be front and center in all of the action. That's why the book of Mark focuses so heavily on the actions of Jesus instead of his sermons.

JOURNAL:

What is the most important thing that God taught you through today's reading?

How can you apply that to your life?

READ: Mark 6-10

AUTHOR: Mark aka John Mark

DATE: AD 55-60 or AD 64-68

AUDIENCE: Christians in Rome

THEME: Jesus as the suffering servant

DAY TWO

JOURNAL:

The first eight chapters of Mark are all about healings, miracles, and casting out demons. Which one of these stories is your favorite? Why?

What is the most important thing that God taught you through today's reading?

How can you apply that to your life?

READ: Mark 11-16

AUTHOR: Mark aka John Mark

DATE: AD 55-60 or AD 64-68

AUDIENCE: Christians in Rome

THEME: Jesus as the suffering servant

DAY THREE

OVERVIEW:

Towards the end of the Gospel, Mark decided to narrow his focus and really display the reason for Christ's arrival in Jerusalem (and on earth in general). Mark gives us the most in-depth look at the final week in all of the Gospels.

Jesus knew what was going to happen, and it wasn't pretty. His life was to be laid down as an exchange for all of the sins of humanity. He actually became sin so we could be seen as sinless. Every disease, every anger issue, every addiction, every evil desire from the past, present, and future were nailed to the cross so we could be set free. What we struggle with today was already taken care of 2,000 years ago. If Jesus is your personal Savior, you are FREE. RIGHT NOW!

JOURNAL:

Have you had a revelation of that concept yet? How does that change the way you live?

What is the most important thing that God taught you through today's reading?

How can you apply that to your life?

READ: Luke 1-3

AUTHOR: Luke the physician

DATE: AD 58-60 or AD 60-62

AUDIENCE: A Roman official or judge named Theophilus

THEME: Christ is the Savior for the Gentiles too

DAY FOUR

OVERVIEW:

When studying the four Gospels, the most important thing that you can do is look at the stories through the eyes of the writer. In this case, Luke is writing to a Roman judge on behalf of his buddy Paul. Therefore, the content is much more focused on how Jesus interacted with Gentiles, Romans, and women…all of which hit home for Jesus.

Luke is a very unique book in the sense that it has many stories that the other authors did not have because they weren't able to interview the right people. Remember, this is being used as a court document and Luke was not present during the ministry of Jesus so he had to get information from all of the eyewitnesses that he could, in order to piece together the proper angle for Paul's pending release. That's why the feel of this book seems a little different compared to the other Gospels.

Luke, being a doctor, approached Jesus from the perspective of the Son of Man, which is why he dated Jesus' genealogy all the way back to the first man, Adam, through the line of Mary.

JOURNAL:

What is the most important thing that God taught you through today's reading?

How can you apply that to your life?

_____

_____

_____

_____

_____

_____

_____

_____

_____

_____

_____

_____

_____

_____

_____

_____

READ: Luke 4-9

AUTHOR: Luke the physician

DATE: AD 58-60 or AD 60-62

AUDIENCE: A Roman official or judge named Theophilus

THEME: Christ is the Savior for the Gentiles too

DAY FIVE

JOURNAL:

Have you ever been tempted like Jesus was in the wilderness? What happened?

The men that Jesus chose as his disciples were almost all teenagers. What do you think it as about Jesus that made all of the men leave their jobs to follow him?

What is the most important thing that God taught you through today's reading?

How can you apply that to your life?

_____
_____
_____
_____
_____
_____
_____
_____
_____
_____
_____
_____
_____
_____
_____
_____
_____
_____
_____
_____
_____
_____
_____
_____
_____

READ: Luke 10-19

AUTHOR: Luke the physician

DATE: AD 58-60 or AD 60-62

AUDIENCE: A Roman official or judge named Theophilus

THEME: Christ is the Savior for the Gentiles too

DAY SIX

JOURNAL:

Is it easy or hard for you to follow along with the parables that Jesus told? Why do you think he explained stuff that way?

What is the most important thing that God taught you through today's reading?

How can you apply that to your life?

READ: Luke 20-24

AUTHOR: Luke the physician

DATE: AD 58-60 or AD 60-62

AUDIENCE: A Roman official or judge named Theophilus

THEME: Christ is the Savior for the Gentiles too

OVERVIEW:

Luke really is a Gospel for everybody. He includes many important stories that we don't read about in the other Gospels. And all of these are used to teach us new things.

Your faith journey and how you have witnessed God move in your life are some of the greatest things that we could ever share with the world. They produce hunger. They produce connection. They can also boost faith in hopes that God will work for us in the same way that He has for others.

JOURNAL:

Write out a simplified version of your life story and how you have witnessed God move through it all:

_____

_____

_____

_____

_____

_____

_____

_____

_____

_____

_____

_____

_____

_____

_____

_____

_____

_____

_____

_____

_____

READ: John 1-5

AUTHOR: The apostle John

DATE: AD 80's

AUDIENCE: Churches around Asia Minor

THEME: Jesus came to give eternal life because he is God

OVERVIEW:

The Gospel of John is 90% unique from the other Gospels as he explores Jesus from the Son of God perspective, including his preexistent genealogy at the beginning of his writing. Whereas the other Gospels looked at what Jesus did and said, John approached his story from the inside by looking at how Jesus felt and who he was as a person. He made it a point to show that Jesus is fully human and fully divine at the same time. There was nothing that Jesus could do while on Earth without

JOURNAL:

Isn't it amazing that the Creator of the universe came down to his creation just to save it? Describe a time when you worked extra hard on a project and it didn't turn out as you planned:

What is the most important thing that God taught you through today's reading?

How can you apply that to your life?

READ: John 6-10

AUTHOR: The apostle John

DATE: AD 80's

AUDIENCE: Churches around Asia Minor

THEME: Jesus came to give eternal life because he is God

OVERVIEW:

One thing to notice in all of John's books is that he writes in sevens. Seven is the number of perfect divinity and is a very important number in the Jewish faith. The top two things that John focuses on in this Gospel are seven major miracles as well as seven "I AM" statements.

JOURNAL:

List the seven miracles that he points out:

1. (John 2:1-11)

2. (John 4:43-54)

3. (John 5:1-9)

4. (John 6:1-14)

5. (John 6:16-21)

6. (John 9:1-33)

7. (John 11:1-44)

What do all of these miracles show you about Jesus?

READ: John 11-17

AUTHOR: The apostle John

DATE: AD 80's

AUDIENCE: Churches around Asia Minor

THEME: Jesus came to give eternal life because he is God

JOURNAL:

As mentioned yesterday, there were also seven "I AM" statements, which meant everything to John. List all seven of them here:

1. (John 6:35)

2. (John 8:12)

3. (John 10:9)

4. (John 10:11)

5. (John 11:25)

6. (John 14:6)

7. (John 15:5)

YOUR PEOPLE
YOUR PEOPLE
YOUR PEOPLE
YOUR PEOPLE
YOUR PEOPLE
YOUR PEOPLE
YOUR PEOPLE
YOUR PEOPLE
YOUR PEOPLE

YOUR GOD
YOUR GOD
YOUR GOD
YOUR GOD
YOUR GOD
YOUR GOD
YOUR GOD
YOUR GOD
YOUR GOD

READ: John 18-21

AUTHOR: The apostle John

DATE: AD 80's

AUDIENCE: Churches around Asia Minor

THEME: Jesus came to give eternal life because he is God

DAY ELEVEN

JOURNAL:

John focused heavily on the fact that Jesus was fully God and fully man at the same time. What amazing news for all of us!

How does that understanding impact your view of Jesus?

What does that mean for your own faith journey?

What is the most important thing that God taught you through today's reading?

How can you apply that to your life?

READ: Acts 1-8

AUTHOR: Luke the physician

DATE: AD 60-62

AUDIENCE: A Roman Official or judge named Theophilus

THEME: The gospel message is for everyone, everywhere

DAY TWELVE

OVERVIEW:

The book of Acts is a historical look at the first 30 years of the early church and, in many cases, could be used as a model for missionary work around the world today.

But one thing to note is that before Paul went on any missionary journeys, he went to his hometown of Tarsus for ten years in order to preach there and build himself up. What about us? Do our hometowns see the fire in each of us? They need to see our changed life before the world will. How can you use Paul as an example regarding hometown missionary work instead of just doing short-term mission trips every once in a while?

JOURNAL:

What is the most important thing that God taught you through today's reading?

How can you apply that to your life?

AUTHOR: Luke the physician

DATE: AD 60-62

AUDIENCE: A Roman Official or judge named Theophilus

THEME: The gospel message is for everyone, everywhere

DAY THIRTEEN

JOURNAL:

Do you think that Paul dealt with any fear during his first time going on a missionary journey?

In Chapter 15, we have the infamous Jerusalem Council. What was the council debating? What was the final consensus? What does that mean for us?

What is the most important thing that God taught you through today's reading?

How can you apply that to your life?

READ: Acts 16-21

AUTHOR: Luke the physician

DATE: AD 60-62

AUDIENCE: A Roman Official or judge named Theophilus

THEME: The gospel message is for everyone, everywhere

DAY FOURTEEN

JOURNAL:

Paul's third missionary journey was a pretty long one that ended up back in Jerusalem. He spent extra time in a lot of the cities mentoring the people on how to live a life dedicated to the Lord.

Do you currently have a mentor? If not, who is someone that you would like to mentor you? I would highly encourage you to reach out to them this week to see if they would mentor you once or twice per month.

What is the most important thing that God taught you through today's reading?

How can you apply that to your life?

READ: Acts 22-28

AUTHOR: Luke the physician

DATE: AD 60-62

AUDIENCE: A Roman Official or judge named Theophilus

THEME: The gospel message is for everyone, everywhere

DAY FIFTEEN

OVERVIEW:

In Chapters 23-26, we see the beginning of Paul's trial. It is the reason why this book was written in the first place. It's Rome vs. Christianity. Paul never harmed anybody on his journeys, he only healed them. So the guards were fairly lenient as they watched over him. Even on the ship heading to Rome, the crew seemed to listen to Paul's prophecies and wisdom as a higher authority than their own common sense.

They all eventually made it to Rome and Paul was placed on house arrest. He was still able to welcome visitors at any time though, and continued to preach the gospel every day. That's where he sat writing letters to the churches which he had built on his journeys while awaiting the trial that was soon to take place.

JOURNAL:

What is the most important thing that God taught you through today's reading?

How can you apply that to your life?

_____

_____

_____

_____

_____

_____

_____

_____

_____

_____

_____

_____

_____

_____

_____

_____

_____

_____

_____

_____

_____

Pauls Missionary Journeys

Your task today is to fill in the blank maps on the next few pages with each route from Paul's three missionary journeys.

FIRST MISSIONARY JOURNEY

1. Antioch
2. Seleucia
3. Salamis
4. Paphos

5. Perga
6. Antioch
7. Iconium
8. Lystra

9. Derbe
10. Lystra
11. Iconium
12. Antioch

13. Perga
14. Attalia
15. Antioch

SECOND MISSIONARY JOURNEY

1. Antioch
2. Tarsus
3. Derbe
4. Lystra
5. Iconium

6. Pisidia
7. Troas
8. Neapolis
9. Philippi
10. Thessalonica

11. Berea
12. Athens
13. Corinth
14. Cenchrea
15. Ephesus

16. Paphos
17. Caesarea
18. Jerusalem
19. Caesarea
20. Antioch

THIRD MISSIONARY JOURNEY

1 Antioch
2. Tarsus
3. Iconium
4. Ephesus
5. Troas

6. Philippi
7. Thessalonica
8. Corinth
9. Thessalonica
10. Philippi

11. Troas
12. Assos
13. Miletus
14. Patara
15. Tyre

16. Ptolemais
17. Caesarea
18. Jerusalem

READ: Romans 1-8

AUTHOR: The apostle Paul

DATE: AD 55-56

AUDIENCE: The church in Rome

THEME: Basics of Christianity and Jew/Gentile relations

DAY SEVENTEEN

OVERVIEW:

Romans is the gospel. It's a letter written by the apostle Paul about grace and redemption. This is God's plan for humanity. Therefore, it is extremely important that you take time to really understand this book. It's my prayer that God gives you a revelation of your new identity over the next couple days. As a believer in Jesus, you are now a saint. Sin has been rendered powerless because of what Jesus did for you...and me!

JOURNAL:

What does it mean to be a saint? How does that make you feel knowing that God now views you as a saint?

What is the most important thing that God taught you through today's reading?

How can you apply that to your life?

READ: Romans 9-11

AUTHOR: The apostle Paul

DATE: AD 55-56

AUDIENCE: The church in Rome

THEME: Basics of Christianity and Jew/Gentile relations

DAY EIGHTEEN

JOURNAL:

These chapters talk a lot about Israel. Once we dive into the Old Testament later, you'll see that God still has a great plan for his people and the country of Israel. What do you know about Israel today?

What is the most important thing that God taught you through today's reading?

How can you apply that to your life?

READ: Romans 12-16

AUTHOR: The apostle Paul

DATE: AD 55-56

AUDIENCE: The church in Rome

THEME: Basics of Christianity and Jew/Gentile relations

DAY NINETEEN

OVERVIEW:

The New Testament teaches us that we are supposed to be everything that Jesus was as a man. We are in covenant with God, so all of those things are now a part of our nature. If we don't walk them out, then we are acting against our nature.

Jesus was fully God AND fully man, which means that he had to make the same moment-by-moment decisions that we do. That should give us confidence!

JOURNAL:

In what ways would you like to be more like Jesus?

What is the most important thing that God taught you through today's reading?

How can you apply that to your life?

READ: 1 Corinthians 1-6

AUTHOR: The apostle Paul

DATE: AD 55-56

AUDIENCE: The church in Corinth

THEME: Love is the reason for everything

DAY TWENTY

OVERVIEW:

From what we can gather in 1 and 2 Corinthians, we learn Paul had actually written four letters to the church of Corinth...two of which we have, two of which were lost.

In this first letter, Paul addresses different practical issues within the church such as spiritual gifts, how to love well, and what they were allowed to eat.

JOURNAL:

What is the most important thing that God taught you through today's reading?

How can you apply that to your life?

READ: 1 Corinthians 7-11

AUTHOR: The apostle Paul

DATE: AD 55-56

AUDIENCE: The church in Corinth

THEME: Love is the reason for everything

DAY TWENTY ONE

JOURNAL:

What is the most important thing that
God taught you through today's reading?

How can you apply that to your life?

_____
_____
_____
_____
_____
_____
_____
_____
_____
_____
_____
_____
_____
_____
_____
_____
_____
_____
_____
_____
_____
_____
_____
_____

READ: 1 Corinthians 12-16

AUTHOR: The apostle Paul

DATE: AD 55-56

AUDIENCE: The church in Corinth

THEME: Love is the reason for everything

DAY TWENTY TWO

OVERVIEW:

In the middle of Chapters 12-14, Paul writes what is known as the "love chapter". He does that deliberately to teach that loving others is the main focus behind every spiritual gift. If you are exercising your gifts for any other reason you might as well not even use them. Love should be the reason behind everything.

JOURNAL:

How could you show more love to those around you every day?

What is the most important thing that God taught you through today's reading?

How can you apply that to your life?

DAY TWENTY THREE

THERE ARE FOUR MAIN VIEWS ON SPIRITUAL GIFTS TODAY:

Cessationist: Spiritual gifts were only for the early church and are not relevant today.

Continuationist: Spiritual gifts are for today, but the "sign" gifts need to be looked at and tested with caution.

Charismatic: Spiritual gifts are for every generation, and they should be practiced today. This view is limited by Scripture with no additions to the Word.

Hyper Charismatic: Spiritual gifts are for every generation and contemporary revelations are equal to Scripture.

JOURNAL:

Which view on gifts do you associate with? Why?

_____
_____
_____
_____
_____
_____
_____
_____
_____
_____
_____
_____
_____
_____
_____
_____
_____
_____
_____
_____

The Break Down

Spiritual gifts are not to be confused with natural talent. Every Christian has at least one spiritual gift, if not multiple. Not Christian has every spiritual gift. The Holy Spirit chooses which gifts each of us receive. God's will is not accomplished if love is not the main motivation behind the gifts.

PROPHECY:

Prophecy is the ability to speak truth into an individual's destiny and to reveal future events to the church in order to call for repentance or build them up. People with this gift can easily read others and "just know" things before they happen.

TEACHING:

Teaching is the ability to apply Scripture in an easy-to-understand way. People with this gift love to study and are very focused on doctrinal application.

GIVING:

Giving is the ability to earn money in order to meet the needs of others in a cheerful manner. People with this gift are good at making money and like to give behind the scenes.

MERCY:

Mercy is the desire to take care of those that are going through difficult times without expecting anything in return. People with this gift enjoy one-on-one serving and are able to sympathize naturally.

SERVICE:

Service is the ability to meet physical needs within the body of Christ and apply a spiritual significance to it. People with this gift like to work behind the scenes and get joy out of helping others.

ENCOURAGEMENT:

Encouragement is the ability to motivate others on their faith journey. People with this gift are good counselors and can personally apply Scripture.

LEADERSHIP:

Leadership is the ability to direct others in completing a God-given task or specific ministry work. People with this gift can clearly share a vision and others gladly follow their lead.

APOSTLESHIP:

Apostles are those that have a desire to be sent out to start churches and ministries in the local community and around the world. People with this gift are comfortable in other cultures and able to execute a specific vision.

EVANGELISM:

Evangelists are those that can easily share the gospel with unbelievers and lead them to a personal relationship with Jesus Christ. People with this gift are very personable and convincing of the Truth.

WISDOM:

Wisdom is the ability to look at a situation and advise the best strategy for action based on the insight given. People with this gift can see various outcomes and can discern which one is the best to take.

FAITH:

Faith is the ability to have an overly confident belief that God will accomplish the impossible despite reality. People with this gift trust God completely and act in confidence.

MIRACLES:

Miracles is the ability to be used as a vessel for God to reveal His power through supernatural acts that alter the natural realm. Miracles are most often used to authenticate the gospel message. People with this gift speak truth with confidence and have it authenticated by a supernatural act.

TONGUES:

There are three different types of tongues: One is a private prayer language (1 Cor 14:14-15), another is the ability to speak out a divine message in a new language in order for the Body to be built up, and the third is an entire language as a gift, which is to be used for missionary work.

PASTORS:

Pastors are those that can guide, counsel, protect, and disciple a group of believers. Many times this gift is joined with the gift of teaching. People with this gift are great leaders and have a heart for discipleship.

KNOWLEDGE:

Knowledge is the ability to understand the Word and make it relevant to the church or specific situations. This gift includes supernatural words of knowledge that are to be used in serving others. People with this gift are able to seek out truth in the Bible and typically have unusual insight into situations or a person's life.

HEALING:

Healing is the ability to be used as a vessel by God in order to cure sickness and restore health back to normal. People with this gift are able to demonstrate the power of God through prayer, the laying on of hands or a spoken word.

DISCERNMENT (DISTINGUISHING OF SPIRITS):

Discernment is the ability to perceive what is from God through the discernment of good and evil spirits. People with this gift can easily tell what is from God and what is counterfeit.

INTERPRETING OF TONGUES:

Interpreting of tongues is the ability to translate a language that the hearer doesn't know whether it is a real language or a heavenly language.

JOURNAL:

Describe a time when you feel like God used you, whether you knew it was your spiritual gift or not.

What is the purpose of spiritual gifts? (1 Peter 4:10-11)

After looking at all of the gifts, which gift(s) do you think you might have?

Can you think of a way to exercise your gift(s) in order to grow in it / them?

_____

_____

_____

_____

_____

_____

_____

_____

_____

_____

_____

_____

_____

_____

_____

_____

_____

_____

_____

_____

_____

_____

_____

READ: 2 Corinthians 1-7
AUTHOR: The apostle Paul
DATE: AD 55-56
AUDIENCE: The church in Corinth
THEME: Victory in Christ

OVERVIEW:

While the first letter to the Corinthians dealt with practical issues within the church, the second letter deals with personal insults that forced Paul to stand up for himself.

We know that a group of "super apostles" came into Corinth once Paul left, and they tried to take over by building themselves up and pushing Paul down. We don't know who they were exactly, but the content suggests that they were Jewish.

Some of the attacks on his character were that he wasn't bold enough, that he didn't care for the Corinthians since he was in a different city, that he wasn't a good speaker and that he wasn't even qualified to be teaching them such things. The "super apostles" knew that if they attacked Paul, his message would be thrown out as well. This is his rebuttal.

JOURNAL:

Explain a time when you have had someone attack your character. How did you handle it?

What is the most important thing that God taught you through today's reading?

How can you apply that to your life?

READ: 2 Corinthians 8-13
AUTHOR: The apostle Paul
DATE: AD 55-56
AUDIENCE: The church in Corinth
THEME: Victory in Christ

DAY TWENTY FIVE

OVERVIEW:

Right in the middle of his encouragement and defense, Paul includes a large section on collecting money to give to the poor in Jerusalem. What?? We know from the past that Paul has a major heart for the poor so that makes sense, but doesn't that seem a little random? Well the Corinthians knew the importance of love, considering the whole chapter on it in his previous letter to them. It was a part of the gospel and therefore a part of their life. The "super apostles" weren't teaching love. They were attacking Paul and focusing on the negative instead. Paul knew that if he focused on loving others through donating to the poor then they would turn towards the truth. And this approach worked because we know that his third visit to Corinth was a joyous one.

JOURNAL:

What are some ways that you can better serve the poor?

What is the most important thing that God taught you through today's reading?

How can you apply that to your life?

READ: Galatians 1-3
AUTHOR: The apostle Paul
DATE: AD 48 or AD 55
AUDIENCE: The churches in Galatia
THEME: Freedom through Christ alone

DAY TWENTY SIX

OVERVIEW:

The vibe of Galatians is much more negative compared to most of Paul's other letters because of how serious he feels about being set free from the Law. There is no joking around with him on that matter. Freedom is everything.

The Jewish people were being strangled by the Law. There was no way to fulfill it, but they still did their best to gain God's approval. Paul shows them how times have changed.

Galatians 2:20 says, "I have been crucified with Christ. It is no longer I who live, but Christ who lives in me. And the life I now live in the flesh I live by faith in the Son of God, who loved me and gave himself for me" (ESV). What do you think Paul meant when he said it was no longer he who lived, but rather Christ who lived in him? How can you apply that to your own life?

JOURNAL:

What is the most important thing that God taught you through today's reading?

How can you apply that to your life?

_____
_____
_____
_____
_____
_____
_____
_____
_____
_____
_____
_____
_____
_____
_____
_____
_____
_____
_____
_____

READ: Galatians 4-6

AUTHOR: The apostle Paul

DATE: AD 48 or AD 55

AUDIENCE: The churches in Galatia

THEME: Freedom through Christ alone

DAY TWENTY SEVEN

OVERVIEW:

Instead of getting so caught up in what we should and shouldn't do, I believe that we need to redirect our attention to our identity in Christ and who God says we are. Galatians 4:6-7 says, "And because you are sons, God has sent the Spirit of His Son into our hearts, crying, 'Abba! Father!' So you are no longer a slave, but a son, and if a son, then an heir through God" (ESV).

Because of what Jesus did, you are an heir to the throne and have received the exact same inheritance that Jesus received. This. Is. HUGE. That means God blesses YOU the same way that He blessed His Son, JESUS. With salvation, providing for our needs, understanding the Father's heart, joy, gifts, communication with God, answered prayers, etc. Our inheritance was already paid for so God is literally just waiting for you to accept it. He gets joy out of blessing you. So take it in!

JOURNAL:

How have you seen God's blessing on your life? How can you better walk in this new understanding?

What is the most important thing that God taught you through today's reading?

How can you apply that to your life?

READ: Ephesians 1-3

AUTHOR: The apostle Paul

DATE: AD 60-62

AUDIENCE: The church in Ephesus

THEME: Walking in your new identity

DAY TWENTY EIGHT

OVERVIEW:

Paul begins Ephesians by saying, "Long before he laid down earth's foundations, he had us in mind, had settled on us as the focus of his love, to be made whole and holy by his love. Long, long ago he decided to adopt us into his family through Jesus Christ…He wanted us to enter into the celebration of his lavish gift-giving by the hand of his beloved Son" (1:4-6 MSG). There is so much about our new identity in this little section along! We have been adopted. We are to be made whole and holy. His desire is to bless us. Those are all amazing things! Ephesians is all about our identity and how we are different now that we are believers.

JOURNAL:

What does it mean to be adopted into the Kingdom?

What does it mean to be made whole and holy?

What is the most important thing that God taught you through today's reading?

How can you apply that to your life?

READ: Ephesians 4-6

AUTHOR: The apostle Paul

DATE: AD 60-62

AUDIENCE: The church in Ephesus

THEME: Walking in your new identity

OVERVIEW:

Paul tells us to be imitators of God in Chapter 5. In other words, our lives should reflect Jesus. That means it is our job to bring the kingdom of God into our everyday life. Some people have such a hard time trying to figure out what the will of God is. I believe that the overarching will of God, after we receive His Son, is to bring heaven to earth and to ruin the works of the devil every day (1 John 3:8b). That's it!

JOURNAL:

How can you ruin the works of the devil in your daily life?

In Chapter 6, Paul describes the Armor of God and teaches us the keys to success regarding spiritual warfare.

Have you ever dealt with spiritual warfare before? What happened?

READ: Philippians 1-4

AUTHOR: The apostle Paul

DATE: AD 61-62

AUDIENCE: The church in Philippi

THEME: Joy in the Lord

OVERVIEW:

The letter to the Philippians can be put in the category of "Prison Epistles", alongside Ephesians, Colossians, and Philemon. Philippians was written after those three as Paul was ending his stint under Roman house arrest. Paul had been told of issues among the Philippians by a gentleman named Epaphroditus who was sent to Paul as somewhat of a housekeeper. This letter was a response to those issues and a promise that Epaphroditus would be sent home soon.

JOURNAL:

In 4:4, Paul says, "Rejoice in the Lord always; again I will say, rejoice!" (ESV). What does it mean to rejoice always? How is that even possible?

In which areas of your life do you struggle with remaining joyful?

What is the most important thing that God taught you through today's reading?

How can you apply that to your life?

READ: Colossians 1-4
AUTHOR: The apostle Paul
DATE: AD 60-61
AUDIENCE: The church in Colossae
THEME: Fullness in Christ

OVERVIEW:

As we learned when looking at Ephesians and Philemon, Paul was under Roman house arrest at the time of this writing. During house arrest, he could have visitors and live somewhat freely, all the while chained to a Roman soldier.

A man named Epaphras, who was part of the church in Colossae, reported to Paul that things were going badly. Paul had no real authority over the Colossians, but he did his best to redirect their focus, in order to understand their new self / identity in Christ.

A large portion of Colossians matches the content of Ephesians so this will be a little repetitive, but it helps that Paul writes in a very straight-forward way, so that they understand it.

JOURNAL:

What is the most important thing that God taught you through today's reading?

How can you apply that to your life?before? What happened?

GOALS

First off, you are CRUSHING it! One month down, two to go. Secondly, let's touch base on your goals and adjust accordingly.

Where are you at on your faith journey now?

Did you spend your time wisely this past month?

In what ways can you improve over the next month?

List 3 things that you are thankful for.

_____
_____
_____
_____
_____
_____
_____
_____
_____
_____
_____
_____
_____
_____
_____
_____
_____
_____
_____
_____
_____
_____
_____

READ: 1 Thessalonians 1-5
AUTHOR: The apostle Paul
DATE: AD 50-51
AUDIENCE: The church in Thessalonica
THEME: In expectation of Christ

DAY THIRTY TWO

OVERVIEW:

Paul starts off by commending them for living out their faith so well. You can tell that he is happy with the way that they have been doing things. Paul tends to be a professional motivator. He knows just what to say to get people to progress in their faith. And it works almost every time because they know that he truly cares about them and does it from a place of love. This is a book of encouragement.

JOURNAL:

Who is the most encouraging person that you know? What makes them so encouraging?

What is the most important thing that God taught you through today's reading?

How can you apply that to your life?

READ: 2 Thessalonians 1-3
AUTHOR: The apostle Paul
DATE: AD 50-51
AUDIENCE: The church in Thessalonica
THEME: Comfort until the Second Coming

OVERVIEW:

Second Thessalonians is far different from Paul's first letter to the Thessalonians even though they were written only a few months apart. Paul now seems to be very distant from them and upset over something that was reported to him shortly after the first letter was sent.

He starts off with complimenting them, but quickly gets into the heavy stuff. The Thessalonians had received a false letter from "Paul" saying that the Second Coming was just around the corner so there is no need to work or press-on in their faith anymore. The sad thing is that many people believed it. And

that made Paul furious.

We see the same thing a lot today, not necessarily in the area of work, but definitely in the areas of evangelism and prayer. This should be anything but a time to slow down! We should be ramping up our evangelism and prayer lives more than ever if we truly believe the Second Coming is on the horizon.

If you believe that to be true, what are some things that you can be praying for? And who could you share the good news about Jesus with?

JOURNAL:

What is the most important thing that God taught you through today's reading?

How can you apply that to your life?

_____
_____
_____
_____
_____
_____
_____
_____
_____
_____
_____
_____
_____
_____
_____
_____
_____

READ: 1 Timothy 1-6
AUTHOR: The apostle Paul
DATE: AD 64-66
AUDIENCE: Timothy
THEME: Leadership roles inside of the church

OVERVIEW:

First and Second Timothy and Titus were written by Paul between his final missionary journey and the beginning of his second Roman imprisonment. They are known as the "Pastoral Epistles" because Timothy and Titus were both placed in the pastoral position in different cities, and Paul is teaching them how to get their people in line. He knew that the church had to be in place before any evangelism was to happen. And we all know Paul's thoughts on evangelism: It was everything.

Even though they are called the "Pastoral Epistles", it was neither Timothy nor Titus's job to remain in each location as the pastor. Paul sent them to set things straight, but the main desire of his heart was for them to meet him in Rome before he was martyred.

Timothy was sent to deal with the leadership in Ephesus, but we know that he was a very timid man, making the task far outside of his comfort zone. Titus on the other hand was sent to Crete to deal with the church as a whole (leaders and members), but he was strong and self-sufficient, which made Paul's job much easier.

Not only were these letters used as motivation and direction, but Paul knew that they would also be used as credentials to prove the authority of Timothy and Titus.

JOURNAL:

What is the most important thing that God taught you through today's reading?

How can you apply that to your life?

READ: 2 Timothy 1-4
AUTHOR: The apostle Paul
DATE: Around AD 67
AUDIENCE: Timothy
THEME: Finish strong, Timothy!

DAY THIRTY FIVE

JOURNAL:

Paul's advice to Timothy was to keep pressing on, no matter what happened. He knew that it would all be worth it in the end even though Timothy was beginning to lose hope.

How do you stay strong when times get tough?

What is the most important thing that God taught you through today's reading?

How can you apply that to your life?

READ: Titus 1-3

AUTHOR: The apostle Paul

DATE: Around AD 64-66

AUDIENCE: Titus

THEME: Sound doctrine is everything

OVERVIEW:

Looking good to unbelievers is something that Paul addresses. Believers need to show unbelievers that what we have is better than what they have. We have the answers to all of life's problems. We have the Creator of the universe available 24/7. I believe that the church really needs to improve in this area.

We have separated ourselves so far from society that we often have no idea what would draw unbelievers in. Society portrays us as prude, boring, and hypocritical. Paul says that we must live up to what is good in society's eye and take that one step further. Our goodness and love should draw unbelievers in.

JOURNAL:

What virtues does our culture associate with "good people"? How can we live those out?

What is the most important thing that God taught you through today's reading?

How can you apply that to your life?

READ: Philemon 1
AUTHOR: The apostle Paul
DATE: AD 60-61
AUDIENCE: Philemon
THEME: Forgiveness, equality, and reconciliation in Christ

OVERVIEW:

Philemon is the only personal letter of recommendation in the Bible.

So what is gong on here that makes this book part of Scripture?

Well, back in the day, slavery was much different from what it is today and in the recent past. Whereas our views regarding slavery are all about disrespect and being treated poorly, being a slave in the Greco-Roman world was actually a decent profession. Neither the conditions or the money were bad and there were even more slaves than there were free people. It was a totally acceptable job in terms of conditions and money.

So here we have a man named Onesimus who was a slave of a man named Philemon. Onesimus had run away with a big bag of money, most likely while he was out running an errand for Philemon. We don't know exactly what happened, but we do know that the penalty for running away was death.

Check out the maps of Paul's journeys and locate where Colossae is. Now find Rome. That's how far Onesimus ran so that he wouldn't be found by Philemon. It just so happens to be that while he was in Rome he was introduced to Paul who was on house arrest. During their time together Onesimus gave his life to Christ. Before Onesimus could go any further, Paul made him go back home and ask for forgiveness from Philemon. Yikes. This letter is his appeal.

JOURNAL:

What is the most important thing that God taught you through today's reading?

How can you apply that to your life?

_____
_____
_____
_____
_____
_____
_____
_____
_____
_____
_____
_____
_____
_____
_____

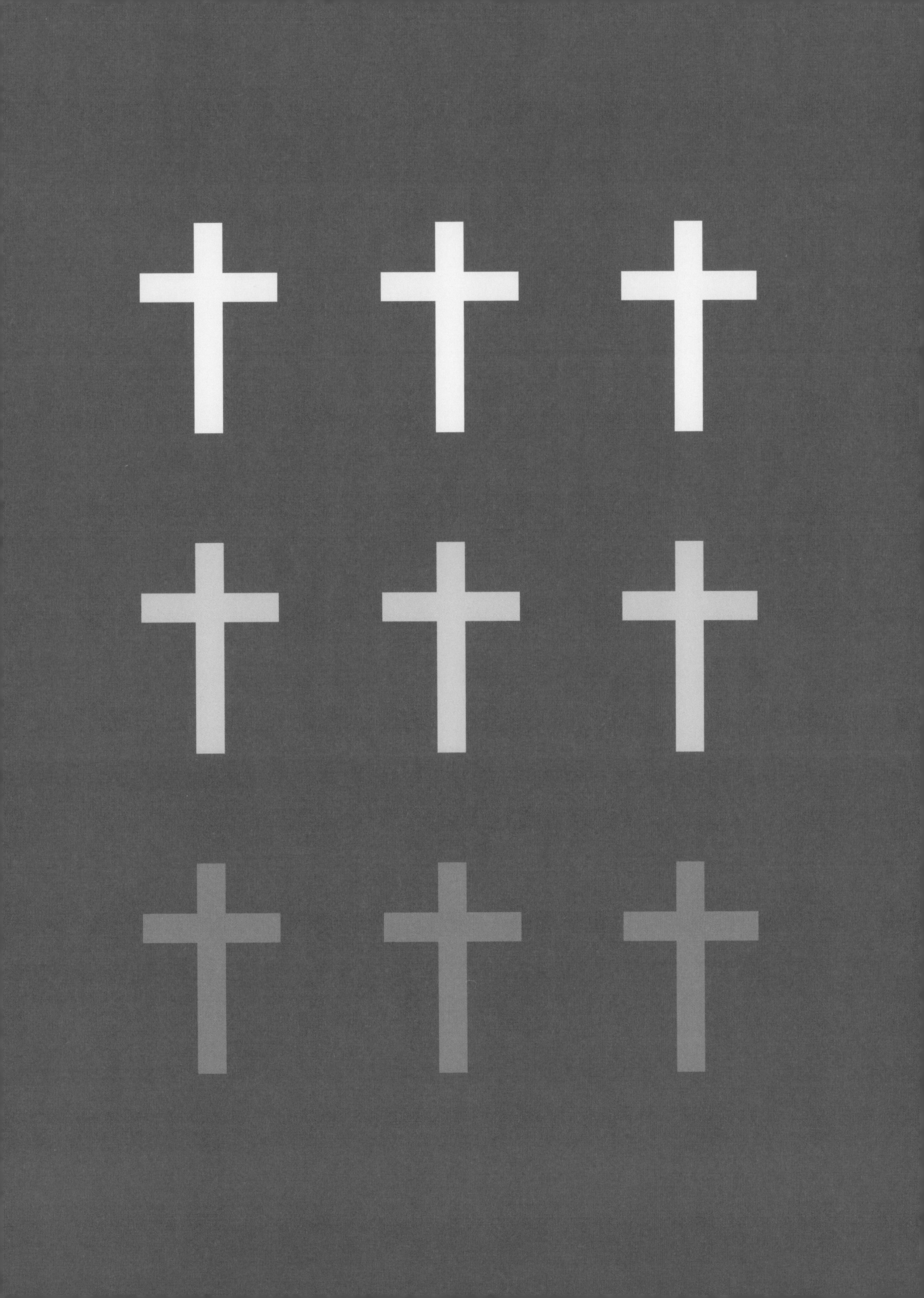

HOLD FIRMLY TO THE TRUTH

READ: Hebrews 1-4

AUTHOR: Unknown

DATE: AD 64-65

AUDIENCE: Hebrew believers

THEME: Jesus is better than Judaism

OVERVIEW:

The reason that the book of Hebrews was written was to show how Jesus and the New Covenant were superior to Judaism and the Law. The author also encouraged the Hebrew believers in their faith journey as they dealt with a new wave of persecution.

Hebrews is not an easy book for many Gentile readers to get through, because of their lack of Old Testament knowledge - that's why it is CRUCIAL to put yourself in the shoes of the reader as best as you can, otherwise your understanding of the context will fall short.

JOURNAL:

In what ways is Jesus better than angels, Moses, and Joshua?

What is the most important thing that God taught you through today's reading?

How can you apply that to your life?

READ: Hebrews 5-10

AUTHOR: Unknown

DATE: AD 64-65

AUDIENCE: Hebrew believers

THEME: Jesus is better than Judaism

DAY THIRTY NINE

JOURNAL:

In what ways is Jesus better than the Aaronic priesthood and the old covenant?

What is the most important thing that God taught you through today's reading?

How can you apply that to your life?

_____
_____
_____
_____
_____
_____
_____
_____
_____
_____
_____
_____
_____
_____
_____
_____
_____
_____
_____
_____
_____
_____
_____
_____
_____

DAY FORTY

OVERVIEW:

Chapter 11 of Hebrews is an unbelievable chapter that displays what many call the "Great Hall of Faith". It's an overview of the most faithful people in Israel's history, including Abraham, Sarah, Jacob, Moses, Rahab, and others. These are the people that set the bar and who we should be looking up to as believers.

JOURNAL:

Who is your role model in Hebrews 11? What can you pull from their life as motivation to grow in your faith?

What is the most important thing that God taught you through today's reading?

How can you apply that to your life?

My role model in Hebrews 11 was noah. God told him to build a boat and noah trusted him even though it hadn't rained in a long time. What gave me motivation in noah's life was, you should just trust in god because it can lead to better things

the most important thing to me was you should always trust in god.

I can apply this to my life by trusting in god even though I dont know whats ahead.

READ: James 1-5

AUTHOR: James, the brother of Jesus

DATE: AD 47-48 or AD 60-62

AUDIENCE: Jews scattered at the

THEME: Faith, works, and wisdom

OVERVIEW:

The book of James is known as the "Proverbs of the New Testament". It's called "Wisdom Literature", which means it is packed with content on how to live your life as a Christian. It's the least doctrinal type of writing, but it is the most practical for day-to-day living.

The five main topics that James looks into are:

Trials

Faith and Works

The Tongue

Wisdom

Wealth

JOURNAL:

Which topic do you struggle the most with? Which topic comes easiest to you?

What is the most important thing that God taught you through today's reading?

How can you apply that to your life?

The thing I most struggle with is trials, I think the easiest topic is the tongue but you can be faced with them all.

The most important thing god taught me was to not be tempted and all good things come through him.

I can apply this to my life by not thinking good things come from anything else but god.

READ: 1 Peter 1-5

AUTHOR: The apostle Peter

DATE: Around AD 64

AUDIENCE: The churches in Asia Minor

THEME: Suffer now and be taken care of later

DAY FORTY TWO

OVERVIEW:

First Peter is a book of persecution and warning for what was to come in the near future as Nero got crazier and crazier.

Who was Nero and what was his deal?

Nero was the Roman Emperor that reigned from AD 54-68. He was an average emperor at the beginning of his reign, but then things took a turn for the worst around AD 64 during the "Great Fire of Rome". The Roman citizens blamed him for starting the first because they knew he had grand plans for the city. And in order to cover his tracks, he blamed the fire on the Christians. From then on, the persecution ramped up in disgusting ways

as Nero did anything to gain popularity. He would torture Christians by crucifying them, using them as entertainment in fights against lions, and most horrifically, soaking them in oil and impaling them on a pole in his garden to be used as a source of light for his dinner parties.

Rome was anything but a pretty sight for Christians. Word was getting out among churches all over the Greco-Roman world so Peter wrote to them in preparation for what was to come. He knew that he would be crucified eventually so this was one of his last forms of contact with them.

JOURNAL:

What is the most important thing that God taught you through today's reading?

How can you apply that to your life?

That you may face obstacles and go through hard times but in the end god will reward you if u are pure and clean.

I can apply this to my life by using this as motivation to stay clean and pure.

READ: 2 Peter 1-3
AUTHOR: The apostle Peter
DATE: AD 47-48 or AD 60-62
AUDIENCE: The churches in Asia Minor
THEME: Watch out for false teachers

OVERVIEW:

Second Peter has a similar layout to 1 Peter in the sense that it focuses on salvation, warnings, and how to deal with what is ahead. Both letters focus on having a strong foundation so that we will not be shaken.

Through God's promises, Peter says that we can be partaker in the divine nature. Peter doesn't say that we become God, like Buddhism or New Age beliefs may suggest, but we are going from glory to glory. Becoming more like Christ every day.

1:5-7 lists a group of qualities that produce more fruit in our lives and transform us into like-mindedness with Christ. They are:

Diligence, moral excellence, knowledge, self-control, perseverance, godliness, brotherly kindness, and love.

JOURNAL:

We should be striving to practice these qualities every single day. What can you do today to increase in each of those qualities? Make a list of what you need to improve on:

What is the most important thing that God taught you through today's reading?

How can you apply that to your life?

READ: 1 John 1-5

AUTHOR: The apostle John

DATE: AD 90-95

AUDIENCE: The churches in Asia Minor

THEME: Security in eternal life

OVERVIEW:

As is apparent in this letter, John sees things in a very black and white manner. Everything in life falls into one of two categories: Good or Evil. You are influenced by both and can choose which one you want to focus on.

Just as we saw in the Gospel of John and will see again in Revelation, John always writes in sevens. He knows the divine importance of the number and follows that structure throughout his main points.

In this letter, he has seven main contrasts that he looks at:

Light and Darkness

Truth and Lies

Loving the Father and Loving the World

Life and Death

Children of God and Children of the Devil

Love and Hate

Good Works and Bad Works

JOURNAL:

What is the most important thing that God taught you through today's reading?

How can you apply that to your life?

READ: 2 John 1
AUTHOR: The apostle John
DATE: AD 90-95
AUDIENCE: Unknown
THEME: Hospitality

OVERVIEW:

We are going to put second and third John together because they are small and fairly self-explanatory. He is telling the two recipients how to be better at showing hospitality. The woman needed to be more cautious and the man needed to be more open.

There were many missionaries going around in the Greco-Roman world, and they were dependent on the hospitality of other believers. That situation allowed for false teaching to spread because anybody that was a "believer" was accepted.

JOURNAL:

Who is the most hospitable person that you know? Why?

What is the most important thing that God taught you through today's reading?

How can you apply that to your life?

READ: 3 John 1

AUTHOR: The apostle John

DATE: AD 90-95

AUDIENCE: A pastor in Asia Minor named Gaius

THEME: Be accepting of other believers

DAY FORTY SIX

JOURNAL:

How can you be more hospitable to other believers?

What is the most important thing that God taught you through today's reading?

How can you apply that to your life?

READ: Jude 1

AUTHOR: Jude, the brother of Jesus

DATE: AD 67-69

AUDIENCE: Believers from the Dispersion

THEME: Contend for the faith

OVERVIEW:

Jude is a book that many people skip over because they don't understand the importance of it. Honestly, it is a pretty strange one. If you compare it to 2 Peter 2, it's almost the same letter, too. Jude addresses a few problems that the audience is facing, which all began with a group of false teachers.

First off, the false teachers were teaching that you could abuse grace. They were saying that once you were saved you could sin all you wanted to and it didn't matter. That's not the Father's heart at all. Yes, grace covers us when we mess up, but our lifestyle should no longer reflect a life of sin. We are new creations and have the power inside of us to live righteously; to go from glory to glory.

Secondly, the false teachers were teaching that Jesus was not the ONLY way to Heaven, but just ONE of the ways. I don't need to explain that one. You know Jesus is the only way (John 14:6)

JOURNAL:

What is the most important thing that God taught you through today's reading?

How can you apply that to your life?

_____
_____
_____
_____
_____
_____
_____
_____
_____
_____
_____
_____
_____
_____
_____
_____
_____

READ: Revelation 1-3
AUTHOR: The apostle John
DATE: Mid-90's
AUDIENCE: To the seven churches
THEME: The current Church and it's future

OVERVIEW:

Revelation has a strange stigma attached to it that causes many people to steer clear from ever attempting to read it. Yet it is the only book in the Bible that promises blessing upon the reader. That's interesting.

Yes, some of the visions may seem weird to us because they aren't the type of thing that we see every day in the natural realm. That's because Revelation is what we call Apocalyptic writing. It looks into the future from the spiritual realm instead of the natural realm perspective. It's the future as God sees it. Revelation completes the story of redemption. We can hold on to the hope for a better tomorrow based on what God's Word says about the future. This is His promise of what will one day be our reality

JOURNAL:

How do you feel about Revelation? Why do you think so many people choose not to study it?

What is the most important thing that God taught you through today's reading?

How can you apply that to your life?

READ: Revelation 4-11

AUTHOR: The apostle John

DATE: Mid-90's

AUDIENCE: To the seven churches

THEME: The current Church and it's future

DAY FORTY NINE

JOURNAL:

What do you think the seven seals and seven trumpets represent?

What is the most important thing that God taught you through today's reading?

How can you apply that to your life?

READ: Revelation 12-16

AUTHOR: The apostle John

DATE: Mid-90's

AUDIENCE: To the seven churches

THEME: The current Church and it's future

JOURNAL:

What do you think the seven bowls represent?

What do you think the mark of the beast will be? Why do you think it is placed on your right arm or forehead?

What is the most important thing that God taught you through today's reading?

How can you apply that to your life?

READ: Revelation 17-22

AUTHOR: The apostle John

DATE: Mid-90's

AUDIENCE: To the seven churches

THEME: The current Church and it's future

DAY FIFTY ONE

JOURNAL:

What do you think the New Earth will be like? What will we eat? What will we do?

What is the most important thing that God taught you through today's reading?

How can you apply that to your life?

YOU DID IT! Congrats! Part one is complete. Now it's time to dig into the Old Testament for the next month. Instead of reading five chapters per day like we did with the New Testament, you will be reading overviews of each book and answering questions based on those - the goal is to get a "big picture" understanding. Then, to finish things off, you will study the Gospel of Matthew to see how everything comes together. But first, let's revisit your goals.

Where are you at on your faith
journey now?

_____
_____
_____

Did you spend your time wisely the past
few weeks?

_____
_____
_____

In what ways can you improve over the
next month?

_____
_____
_____

List 3 things that you are thankful for.

_____
_____
_____
_____
_____
_____
_____
_____
_____

OLD TESTAMENT

FACTS

Torah

Genesis
Exodus
Leviticus
Numbers
Deuteronomy

Historical Narrative

Joshua
Judges
Ruth
1 Samuel
2 Samuel
1 Kings
2 Kings
1 Chronicles
2 Chronicles
Ezra
Nehemiah
Esther

Prophetic Writings

Isaiah
Jeremiah
Lamentations
Ezekiel
Daniel
Hosea
Joel
Amos
Obadiah
Jonah
Micah
Nahum
Habakkuk
Zephaniah
Haggai
Zechariah
Malachi

Wisdom Literature

Job
Psalms
Proverbs
Ecclesiastes
Song of Songs

39 books
Hebrew Language
Creation-400 BC

GENESIS 1-3: THE BEGINNING OF BEGINNINGS

AUTHOR: Moses

DATE: 1446-1406 BC

AUDIENCE: The Israelites

THEME: Creation, the Flood, the Patriarchs, and God's plan of redemption

OVERVIEW:

Genesis is written to God's chosen people, the Israelites. These Israelites have just come out of slavery after 400 years and are being taught their own history through the authorship of this book. Moses – the author – is providing the Israelites with their true heritage and redefining the character of God for his people. Several themes presented throughout Genesis include Creation, the Flood, the Patriarchs, and God's plan for redemption.

Genesis begins with the Creation narrative. God creates the Heavens and the Earth, along with all living organisms over a six-day period. The stages of creation are followed by a final day of rest. At the time of creation, man was formed and given the name, Adam. Adam was placed in the Garden of Eden to work the land, but God instructed him not to eat from one specific tree. God then made woman from one of Adam's ribs and called her Eve. The two tended the Garden together in God's Presence but chose to go against God's orders and ended up eating the forbidden fruit.

JOURNAL:

What did God create / do each day?
(Genesis 1:1-2:3)

Day One:

Day Two:

Day Three:

Day Four:

Day Five:

Day Six:

Day Seven:

Why do you think God created all of this in the first place?

GENESIS 4-11: FALL OF MAN TO TOWER OF BABEL

AUTHOR: Moses

DATE: 1446-1406 BC

AUDIENCE: The Israelites

THEME: Creation, the Flood, the Patriarchs, and God's plan of redemption

OVERVIEW:

As we saw yesterday, Adam and Eve chose to eat the forbidden fruit, which caused God to respond to their disobedience by allowing the curse of hardship and struggle to be placed on humanity. In Christianity, this is called the "Fall of Man" and this rebellion is the birthplace of sin. From that moment forward, Genesis tells of man's continual disobedience towards the will of God.

Times got really dark for a bit and the only righteous people left were a man named Noah and his family. Because of their righteousness, God chose to save Noah's family plus two animals of every kind and basically restarts the human race. I'm sure you've heard this story before – Noah builds an ark and there is a massive flood, wiping humanity (and hopefully sin) out completely. It didn't work.

As time went on, people went off the deep-end again. They decided that they were going to build a tower to reach Heaven and be just like God. Bad idea. When God saw their sin and the intent behind the tower, He scattered the people all across the Earth and scrambled their speech. This time in history was called the "Tower of Babel".

JOURNAL:

Why do you think God chose not to wipe out sin completely and just start over?

I think god decided to not wipe sin complettly out so people can learn from their mistakes and be able to tell right from wrong

GENESIS 12-50: ABRAHAM, ISAAC, JACOB, AND JOSEPH

AUTHOR: Moses

DATE: 1446-1406 BC

AUDIENCE: The Israelites

THEME: Creation, the Flood, the Patriarchs, and God's plan of redemption

OVERVIEW:

In Genesis 12 we get introduced to a man named, Abram, from the land of Haran. God instructs Abram to leave everything behind and start fresh. In doing so, he would be given as many descendants as there are stars in the sky. Even though Abram was really old, he still had faith that God would provide. At that moment, God changes Abram's name to Abraham (meaning "father of many nations") and He gave him and his wife Sarah a son; Isaac.

At one point, when Isaac was a young man, God asked Abraham to sacrifice him. Crazy, right?! But Abraham didn't hesitate to obey God because he knew that God was faithful in his promises, and because of this, God spared Isaac and blessed Abraham. Isaac ended up marrying a woman named Rebekah and they had two sons together; Esau and Jacob. Esau was the older son, and Jacob was the younger.

Jacob went on to father twelve sons, one of which was named Joseph. Joseph was loved by his father Jacob in a special way and the Lord placed a lot of favor on his life. His brothers hated him for it and actually sold him into slavery. Joseph was taken to Egypt to live amongst the Egyptians where he is falsely accused of a crime, imprisoned for a while, and was then set free because God gave him the ability to interpret dreams.

Genesis wraps up with Joseph becoming second in command in Egypt and, through a worldwide famine, he is reunited with his family and everyone is safe and in good health.

JOURNAL:

How can you apply today's overview to your life?

EXODUS OVERVIEW

AUTHOR: Moses

DATE: 1446-1406 BC

AUDIENCE: The Israelites

THEME: Deliverance from slavery and the creation of a nation

OVERVIEW:

Genesis ended with a group of 70 people from the line of Jacob going into Egypt to be saved from a worldwide famine. Exodus picks up 400 years later, and we see what was originally great for them turned into something terrible…slavery. A new Pharaoh entered the scene after Joseph died and he didn't agree with the blessing of the Hebrews, who were now a group of about 2.5 million people total.

The book of Exodus highlights God at work in letting the people go from slavery through ten miraculous plagues. Once they were free, we see miracle after miracle, such as Moses splitting the Red Sea, water coming out of a giant rock in the middle of the desert to quench their thirst, and mana falling from heaven every day so they always had something to eat. Exodus also shows God giving them the Law and how the Israelites were instructed to make sacrifices to God at the Tabernacle.

JOURNAL:

What are the Ten Commandments found in Exodus 20?

Do you still think that God can perform miracles like splitting the Red Sea today?

LEVITICUS OVERVIEW

AUTHOR: Moses

DATE: 1446-1406 BC

AUDIENCE: The Israelites

THEME: Holiness and purification

OVERVIEW:

Leviticus is an instruction manual for how to live a holy life. And it's intense! There were 613 commandments and if you broke ONE of them, you broke them all in God's eyes. Wild. Leviticus also lays out building plans for a Temple that would house the Presence of God and be a place for them to make sacrifices in order to "get right" with God after breaking any of the rules.

It goes super in-depth and a lot of people that don't understand the importance of this book usually skip over it. But MAN, it's important now that we know how Jesus' life, death, and resurrection fulfilled all of the Law, making the commands no longer necessary. Jesus gives us freedom, otherwise we would still be under all of the rules today!

JOURNAL:

With the emphasis on holiness in this book, does your lifestyle reflect holiness? If not, how could it?

What did Jesus have to say about the Law? (Matthew 5:17) How did he update it? (Matthew 5:21-48)

NUMBERS OVERVIEW

AUTHOR: Moses

DATE: 1446-1406 BC

AUDIENCE: The second generation Israelites

THEME: Shows what happens when Israel wanders away from God's plan

OVERVIEW:

If you remember in Exodus, the Israelite people were set free from slavery and were on their way to what was called "The Promised Land" – an area flourishing with vegetation and it was all theirs once they found it. The book of Numbers is a book of rebellion and disappointment. The wanderings were not part of God's plan, but He adjusted to their decisions.

This book is called Numbers because it begins and ends with a census, showing us that Israel was a nation of around 2.5 million people. That's a lot of people wandering through the wilderness together so it's no wonder that rebellion spread among them. Remember, there weren't sound systems or megaphones back then so whatever Moses said had to be passed amongst the people verbally.

Wandering in the wilderness for 40 years was a punishment for not seizing the Promised Land when they had the opportunity. God decided to wait for the first generation to die off so that the second generation had the same opportunity for obedience. The Promised Land was God's will for their lives. The Israelites just needed to have faith and desire it.

JOURNAL:

What does this story show you about the importance of obedience?

Have you ever failed to obey God's plan and, in return, didn't receive your Promised Land...God's best for you? If yes, what happened?

How can you apply today's overview to your life?

_____
_____
_____
_____
_____
_____
_____
_____
_____
_____
_____
_____
_____
_____
_____
_____

NO OTHER NAME

—

JESUS
JESUS
JESUS

DEUTERONOMY OVERVIEW

AUTHOR: Moses

DATE: Around 1406 BC

AUDIENCE: The second generation Israelites

THEME: Covenant renewal with blessings
and curses attached

OVERVIEW:

Many people become confused when they read Deuteronomy for the first time because they don't understand why there is another book in the Torah that dictates the Law. Didn't we just go through the Law when studying Leviticus?! Yes, we did just go over everything, but the audience is different now. The Law was originally given to the first-generation-Israelites that had escaped Egypt. God was so disappointed in their lack of faith that He decided that none of them were going to see the Promised Land. Enter: Their children. This was now a new group of faces that represented Israel and God was giving the nation a fresh start. Before entering the Promised Land, God let them know that they were now going to be held accountable to the covenant, which is why they had to hear about the Law a second time.

Moses gives a blessing over the twelve tribes of Israel and the book concludes with the death of Moses. Now the people are finally able to enter the Promised Land after waiting decades for it.

JOURNAL:

Have you ever waited for something a really long time before being allowed to have it?

What do you think was going through the Israelites minds after waiting so long?

_____

_____

_____

_____

_____

_____

_____

_____

_____

_____

_____

_____

_____

_____

JOSHUA OVERVIEW

AUTHOR: Joshua, Moses's Military General and Assistant

DATE: Around 1390 BC

AUDIENCE: The third generation Israelites

THEME: Possession of the Promised Land

OVERVIEW:

The book of Joshua is the first book out of six that are known as the "Historical Books". The first five books of the Law are complete and now it is time to put everything into action throughout the rest of the Old Testament. Israel's obedience ebbs and flows for the rest of their history, but Joshua shows that they begin on a high note after conquering the Promised Land.

Joshua is in charge of the people now, which would have been a major task to follow in the footsteps of Moses. Just as Moses did, Joshua commanded spies to go and check out Jericho. He only sent two instead of twelve because when Moses sent twelve only two came back with the right word. The spies ended up at a prostitute named Rahab's house, who offered them protection because she believed in their God. In return, the spies said that God would protect her from the destruction of her city, Jericho. Instead of taking over Jericho with power, the Lord commands them to march around the city walls and on the seventh day they were to blow their trumpets. Sounds crazy, but also sounds like the perfect time for God to show up in miraculous ways. And He does. The walls fell down and the Israelites took over the city. After that, they began to conquer the rest of the Promised Land, and Joshua divided the land among the twelve tribes.

JOURNAL:

In what contexts do we read about Rahab in the New Testament? (Matthew 1:5; Hebrews 11:31)

How can you apply today's overview to your life?

JUDGES OVERVIEW

AUTHOR: Unknown, but possibly the prophet Samuel

DATE: 1025-1004 BC

AUDIENCE: The Israelites

THEME: Israel's disobedience and the need to be saved

OVERVIEW:

Before entering the Promised Land, the nation of Israel had one major leader, Moses. The conquest itself was led by one man, Joshua. Now that the Israelites were so spread-out among the Promised Land with specific parameters for each tribe of Israel, they needed to modify the leadership in some way.

Enter: The Judges.

A judge was a deliverer of the people. A hero. A savior. Judges were sent by God as soon as the people cried out for help and their job was to flip the futures back to normal (for at least a short amount of time).

But lo and behold, the people ended up falling back into their sinful ways and "did what was right in their own eyes" instead of what was right in God's eyes. This book outlines the stories of 14 different judges and how the tribe of Benjamin messed up so much that their tribe was reduced to only 600 men.

JOURNAL:

In what areas of your life do you remain "doing what is right in your own eyes" instead of what is right in God's eyes?

What actionable steps can you take to change that?

RUTH OVERVIEW

AUTHOR: Unknown, but possibly the
prophet Samuel

DATE: 1025-1004 BC

AUDIENCE: The Israelites

THEME: Foreshadowing our Kinsman-Redeemer

OVERVIEW:

Ruth is a book of very high importance to the Church. It foreshadows the acceptance of Gentiles (non-Jewish people) within the nation of Israel and is the key that saves them from the time of the judges.

It's a story about a woman named Ruth and how she follows her mother-in-law, Naomi, back to her homeland after Ruth's husband died. Naomi didn't want her to join, but Ruth was persistent. She loved Naomi and wanted to make Naomi's home her home and Naomi's God her God. It was one decision that changed the course of humanity because of who Ruth's descendants ended up becoming.

While Ruth was looking for work, she met a man named Boaz who had the potential to be a great husband. After some time, the two got married and had a son named Obed, who ended up being the grandfather of King David and also an ancestor of Jesus.

JOURNAL:

Have you ever made one small decision that changed your entire life? What was it?

SAMUEL OVERVIEW

AUTHOR: Unkown

DATE: 960-931 BC

AUDIENCE: The Israelites

THEME: Israel's disobedience and the need
The building of a godly monarchy

OVERVIEW:

The books of Samuel cover a period of 150 years of history. That's a lot crammed into a few small books. Originally in the Hebrew Old Testament, they were one big book, but the Greeks split them up in order to be more manageable. For organizational purposes, we are going to look at them combined.

This time period represents a turning point in the history of Israel's leadership as they transition from judges to kings. Samuel is the final judge / prophet, while Saul becomes the first elected king. Everything kind of went downhill from there, until they got to the model king, King David.

Saul couldn't get things under control so God takes His hand of blessing off of him and sends the prophet Samuel to Bethlehem in search of Saul's replacement. Samuel anoints a shepherd-boy named David who would one day take over.

David ended up defeating a giant named, Goliath, with a sling and a stone, which caused Saul to become jealous of David since the people loved him now. Saul's jealousy was so heavy that it ultimately led to his death and David replacing him as king.

David made a lot of mistakes early on, but he was always recognized as a "man after God's own heart". He has a son named Solomon with Bathsheba and Solomon eventually takes over the throne.

JOURNAL:

What do you think it means to be a "man after God's own heart"? How can you be more like that yourself?

_____

_____

_____

_____

_____

_____

_____

_____

_____

_____

_____

_____

KINGS OVERVIEW

AUTHOR: Unknown, but possibly the prophet Jeremiah

DATE: 560-550 BC

AUDIENCE: Jews in exile

THEME: Failing to live for God leads to judgment

OVERVIEW:

Kings is broken down into two different books and it provides a narrative of all the kings that lead the Israelites up until the time of exile. We see good kings, bad kings, and so-so kings, but in the end, there was a downfall that led to the major world power at the time, Assyria, capturing all of the people and bringing them into slavery.

The book of Kings starts off with the great King Solomon, King David's son, uniting the Israelites together. Once he died, the kingdom split into two groups, the northern and southern kingdoms. The north, aka "Israel", consisted of ten of the tribes joining forces, while the south, aka "Judah", only consisted of two tribes.

Even though the southern kingdom was small, they had three very important things going for them: The city of Jerusalem, the temple, and the bloodline of David. For these reasons, they lasted over 100 years longer than the northern kingdom. They definitely weren't perfect, but they had far more good kings than the north.

JOURNAL:

What do you think it was about the city of Jerusalem, the temple, and the bloodline of David that allowed the southern kingdom to last 100 years longer than the northern kingdom?

How can you apply today's overview to your life?

CHRONICLES OVERVIEW

AUTHOR: Unknown, but Jewish tradition states Ezra

DATE: 450-440 BC

AUDIENCE: The returned exile

THEME: The kings of Judah and God's covenant with David's household

OVERVIEW:

Chronicles is also split into two books and, in many instances, recalls a lot of the same content from the books of Kings. This brings up the question – why would you put all of these stories back-to-back? Well in the Hebrew Bible these two sets of books are split-up. Chronicles is actually the last book that they read, so their Bible ends on a happier note than ours does with Malachi.

The thing that makes Chronicles stand out from the pack is that Ezra keeps his focus on the royal line of David and their religious history, whereas Kings focuses on their political history.

Ezra focuses almost solely on the southern kingdom because that was where the temple was located, and his priestly calling connected him to the goodness of the Law and the importance of the temple. He spent his time writing about eight main kings that positively impacted the nation.

Tomorrow we are going to do a timeline that lays all of the history out clearly for you to reference once we dig into the prophets. Stay tuned!

JOURNAL:

Just as Ezra did, list some positive defining moments from your past below, and try to focus on those when the enemy, Satan, tries to condemn you for your failures.

DAY SIXTY FOUR

Instead of going through a specific book today, we are going to do a timeline of the Kings, Prophets, and Major Events. You will find a list of dates, names, and events on the next few pages.

Then, the following pages have a blank timeline on them so it is your job to fill in the names / events and color code the kings as to whether they were Good, Bad, or So-So.

Prophets

Obadiah: 850 BC

Joel: 835–796 BC

Jonah: 770–750 BC

Amos: 760 BC

Hosea: 750–715 BC

Isaiah: 700–680 BC

Micah: 700–686 BC

Nahum: 663–612 BC

Zephaniah: 640–621 BC

Jeremiah: 626–585 BC

Habakkuk: 609–605 BC

Ezekiel: 593–571 BC

Daniel: 530 BC

Haggai: 520 BC

Zechariah: 520–518 BC

Malachi: 430 BC

Events

Divided Kingdom: 930 BC

Fall of Sameria: 722 BC

Fall of Nineveh: 612 BC

First Battle of Carchemish: 609 BC

Second Battle of Carchemish: 606 BC

Second Deportation: 597 BC

Fall of Jerusalem: 586 BC

Fall of Babylon: 539 BC

Cyrus' Decree: 538 BC

First Return: 536 BC

Temple Finished: 516 BC

Second Return: 458 BC

Third Return: 444 BC

Key Kings

Saul: 1050–1010 BC		Bad
David: 1010–970 BC		Good
Solomon 970–930 BC		So-So

Northern Kings

Jeroboam: 930–909 BC	Bad
Nadab: 909–908 BC	Bad
Baasha: 908–886 BC	Bad
Elah: 886–885 BC	Bad
Zimri: 885 BC	Bad
Tibni: 885–880 BC	Bad
Omri: 885–874 BC	Bad
Ahab: 874–853 BC	Bad
Ahaziah: 853–852 BC	Bad
Jeroram: 852–841 BC	Bad
Jehu: 841–814 BC	Bad
Jehoahaz: 814–798 BC	Bad
Jehoash: 798–793 BC	Bad
Jeroboam: 793–753 BC	Bad
Zechariah: 753 BC	Bad
Shallum: 752 BC	Bad
Menahem: 752–742 BC	Bad
Pekahiah: 752–732 BC	Bad
Pekah: 742–740 BC	Bad
Hoshea: 732–723 BC	Bad

Southern Kings

Rehoboam: 930–913 BC	Bad
Abijam: 913–910 BC	Bad
Asa 910–869 BC	Good
Jehoshaphat: 872–848 BC	Good
Jehoram: 853–841 BC	Bad
Ahaziah: 841 BC	Bad
Athaliah: 841–835 BC	Bad
Joash: 835–796 BC	So-So
Amaziah: 796–767 BC	So-So
Azariah / Uzziah: 767–750 BC	So-So
Jotham: 750–732 BC	So-So
Ahaz: 732–725 BC	Bad
Hezekiah: 725–686 BC	Good
Manasseh: 687–642 BC	So-So
Amon: 642–640 BC	Bad
Josiah: 640–609 BC	Good
Jehoahaz: 609 BC	Bad
Jehoiakim: 609–598 BC	Bad
Jehoiachin: 598–597 BC	Bad
Zedekiah: 597–586 BC	Bad

NORTH

930-909 · 909-908 · 908-886 · 886-885 · 885 · 885-880 · 885-874 · 874-853 · 853-852 · 852-841 · 841-814 · 814-798 · 798-793 · 793-753 · 753 · 752

PROPHETS

1050-1010 · 1010-970 · 970-930 · 850 · 835-796 · 770-750 · 760

SOUTH

930-913 · 913-910 · 910-869 · 872-848 · 853-841 · 841 · 841-835 · 835-798 · 796-767 · 767-750

930

BAD KING

GOOD KING

SO-SO KING

NORTH

752-
742

752-
732

742-
740

732-
723

PROPHETS

430

520

530

593-571

520-518

626-585

609-605

663-612

640-621

700-680

700-686

750-715

750-732

597-
586

598-
597

609-
598

609

640-
609

642-
640

687-
642

725-
686

732-
725

750-732

SOUTH

444

458

516

536

538

539

586

597

606

609

612

722

JOB OVERVIEW
AUTHOR: Unknown
DATE: Around 2000 BC
AUDIENCE: Unknown
THEME: Dealing with suffering in the lives of the righteous

OVERVIEW:

The book of Job begins with God allowing Satan to test Job's devotion to Him for a period of time because of God's confidence in Job's steady character. The key here is that Satan always needs permission before he touches the righteous. That is very good news for you and me! Every point of suffering means God allows it because He has confidence that we will persevere. It's always to prove Satan wrong.

After Job's health is attacked, his wife tries to convince Job to curse God, but he won't do it. This led to a dialogue between Job and his friends that basically turns into a lot of bad advice being handed out by these "friends". Finally, God has a conversation with Job where He chooses to restore everything that was taken from him. This restoration came after God humbled Job and taught him that he won't always understand what He is doing in his life.

JOURNAL:

Have you ever suffered? What happened?

How does this new understanding from Job alter your views of what you went through?

Do you know anybody that has fallen away from their faith because of a trial they went through and, in return, ended up blaming God for it? What would you say to them?

_____
_____
_____
_____
_____
_____
_____
_____
_____
_____
_____
_____
_____
_____
_____
_____
_____
_____

PSALMS OVERVIEW

AUTHOR: Many individuals including King David, Moses, and Solomon

DATE: Collection from over 1000 years

AUDIENCE: Varied, but mainly the Israelites

THEME: God is good all the time

OVERVIEW:

The book of Psalms is the longest book in the Bible and the easiest to relate to. Every psalm was written from an emotional state that we deal with today, whether that's joy, love, thankfulness, anger, etc. These psalms were used as a devotional for the Jewish people, yet, they are also for you and me. They're bite-sized and we can hold tightly to their truths no matter what we are going through.

JOURNAL:

Today I would encourage you to write one of your own psalms / poems below, covering any topic that can be found throughout the Psalms. Ex. Creation, joy, prayer, love, the Messiah, peace, war, anger, thankfulness, worship, praise, judgment, hope, trust, glory, etc.

THE PSALMS AR
THE PSALMS AR
THE PSALMS AR
THE PSALMS AR
THE PSALMS AR
THE PSALMS AR
THE PSALMS AR
THE PSALMS AR

GOOD

FOR

YOU

THE PSALMS AR
THE PSALMS AR
THE PSALMS AR
THE PSALMS AR
THE PSALMS AR

PROVERBS OVERVIEW

AUTHOR: King Solomon, Hezekiah's men, Agur and Lemuel

DATE: Written 990-931 BC and edited around 700 BC

AUDIENCE: Young, wise men of Israel

THEME: Sharing wisdom

DAY SIXTY SEVEN

OVERVIEW:

In 2nd Chronicles 1, God asked Solomon what he wanted in life. Instead of saying wealth or honor like most people would pick, Solomon chose to be granted wisdom and knowledge. Because of his choice, "God answered Solomon, 'Because this was in your heart, and you have not asked for possessions, wealth, honor, or the life of those who hate you, but have asked for wisdom and knowledge for yourself that you may govern my people over whom I have made you king, wisdom and knowledge are granted to you. I will also give you riches, possessions, and honor, such as none of the kings had who were before you, and none after you shall have the like.'" (11-12 ESV).

Solomon was the wisest person to ever live and we should be forever grateful that he left us with a collection of 900 proverbs on how to live a good life. How cool is that?!

JOURNAL:

If God asked you what you wanted in life, what would you say?

In your opinion, what is the "good life"?

Do you have a favorite proverb? If so, what is it?

_____

_____

_____

_____

_____

_____

_____

_____

_____

_____

_____

_____

ECCLESIASTES OVERVIEW

AUTHOR: King Solomon

DATE: 940-931 BC

AUDIENCE: The wise Israelites of the time

THEME: Everything under the sun is vanity

OVERVIEW:

As we know, King Solomon was the definition of what society deemed as successful. He was the wisest, richest person to ever live, and people traveled thousands of miles just to witness his grandeur. He was the MAN.

But even though he had the world at his fingertips, it still didn't satisfy his appetite. In fact, he felt like he had wasted his life just by pursuing meaningless things. Some of you may be in the same boat and / or some of you may have actually come to the Lord while searching out a deeper meaning for this thing called life. That's my story.

Solomon talks a lot about how material things fade away and that real life is only found in the things that God provides. It's basically a warning against pursuing things that are temporary.

JOURNAL:

What would you say is the meaning of life?

Do you think this means all material things are bad? How can material things be used for good?

SONG OF SOLOMON OVERVIEW

AUTHOR: Most likely King Solomon

DATE: Around 950 BC

AUDIENCE: The Israelites

THEME: God's view of marriage and sex

OVERVIEW:

Song of Songs was written to show the importance of a godly marriage and how a romantic relationship should progress over time. It shows a dance among partners between pursuing and being pursued. What society tells us is right doesn't actually look anything like the true intimacy that is associated with a godly relationship.

While the media shows what is "acceptable" in relationships and how a couple is supposed to function in their eyes, how are we as Christians called to act? The sad truth is that many times you can't tell the difference between the two. In reality, we are called to be holy. To be set apart. And this book gives an example of what that looks like.

JOURNAL:

Explain a time when you pursued someone or they pursued you. Was it done in a godly way?

What do you think it means to put God at the center of a romantic relationship?

GOALS

HEY! I'm so proud of you. Only twenty more days to go. YOU GOT THIS! Let's revisit those goals quick.

Where are you at on your faith journey now?

Did you spend your time wisely the past few weeks?

In what ways can you improve over the next month?

List 3 things that you are thankful for.

_____
_____
_____
_____
_____
_____
_____
_____
_____
_____
_____
_____
_____
_____
_____
_____
_____
_____
_____
_____
_____
_____

JOEL OVERVIEW

AUTHOR: The prophet Joel

DATE: 835-796 BC

AUDIENCE: The people in Jerusalem

THEME: The Day of the Lord will bring judgment if they do not repent

OVERVIEW:

The book of Joel is a classic prophecy of destruction against Israel, but he uses the imagery of a locust plague coming to take over. Israel most likely endured a massive locust attack that wiped them out for a good amount of time and that is what caused Joel to begin this prophecy – so the people understood where he was coming from.

Joel was begging the people to turn from their ways and fast as a nation. The Lord is always faithful to His word. And He loves giving second chances, even when people don't deserve it. So, Judah's fate lay in their own hands

JOURNAL:

Have you ever fasted? What are your thoughts on fasting?

Have you ever been given a second chance even though you didn't deserve it? What happened?

_____

_____

_____

_____

_____

_____

_____

_____

_____

_____

_____

_____

_____

_____

_____

_____

OBADIAH OVERVIEW
AUTHOR: The prophet Obadiah
DATE: 850 BC or 586 BC
AUDIENCE: The Judahites
THEME: Edom will be judged

OVERVIEW:

Obadiah may be the shortest book in the Old Testament, but it sure has a lot to say about Judah's enemy, Edom. The nation of Edom is actually located within the boundaries of the Promised Land, but Israel had yet to occupy it. The Edomites had attacked the Judahites, which led to a lot of anger in the eyes of Judah. So, Obadiah was prophesying about how the Edomites will eventually get a piece of their own medicine. God had promised to protect His people, so He wasn't going to let a small nation like Edom walk all over them.

One of the biggest reasons that Edom was being judged by God in this book was because of their pride. Edom thought they were the greatest and did everything they could to prove it. That seems to be the case time and time again in these prophetic books.

JOURNAL:

Do you struggle with pride? Spend some time in prayer, and ask God to show you places in your life that are holding you back from being truly humble. Then ask God to forgive you of any pride and to reveal to you a plan of attack in order to defeat it.

JONAH OVERVIEW

AUTHOR: The prophet Jonah

DATE: 770-750 BC

AUDIENCE: The northern kingdom

THEME: Running from God and eventual revival

OVERVIEW:

This prophetic book is far different from the others considering it talks about Jonah's experience instead of a prophecy. Jonah was a very patriotic prophet of the northern kingdom. He often preached repentance, yet hoped for doom towards his enemies, especially the great city of Nineveh.

Nineveh was the capital of Assyria, and basically the pagan capital of the world - housing over one million people. It was not a city to mess with. And they were also the greatest enemy of Israel. Since Jonah was so patriotic, having God tell him to go to his enemies would have been the last thing he wanted to do. So, when God called Him, he ran away because he wanted Nineveh to be judged by God.

Jonah didn't make it too far before God whipped up a storm in order to get his attention and was actually eaten by a giant fish, who later threw him up on the shores of Nineveh. Out of his stubbornness, Jonah preached judgment (instead of repentance) to the king of Nineveh and the entire nation ended up turning from their ways, even though they didn't know God.

JOURNAL:

Have you ever tried to run from God? What was the outcome? How can Jonah's experience be a story of hope for your life?

Do you think non-believers today know when they are doing something wrong? What do they use to gauge their goodness / wrongdoing?

HOSEA OVERVIEW

AUTHOR: Hosea, a citizen of the northern kingdom

DATE: 755-715 BC

AUDIENCE: The northern kingdom

THEME: God's faithfulness to the covenant even when His people fell away

OVERVIEW:

Hosea's prophecy is the final cry of repentance for the northern kingdom. He was the last one that we see before they fall into the hands of Assyria. This message of romantic imagery was not enough to turn their hearts around.

Hosea starts off with a story of his love life. God then takes that story and spins it into His passionate love for the people of Israel. You see, Hosea's wife was a prostitute that was stuck in her ways. Even though she was loved by her husband she still chose to fall back into the evil ways of the world. God told Hosea to chase after her with unwavering love.

You see, God loved the people of Israel unconditionally. They were His pride and joy even though they didn't live it out. Instead of God using Hosea as a vessel to share His anger, God shared His love through a personal experience, which made the prophecy hit home even harder for Hosea.

JOURNAL:

What do you think was going through Hosea's mind when God told him to chase after his wife? At this point do you think he truly still loved her? Or was he just doing it out of obedience?

Has God ever challenged you to love someone that has betrayed you? If so, what happened?

AMOS OVERVIEW

AUTHOR: A poor shepherd named Amos

DATE: Around 760 BC

AUDIENCE: The northern kingdom

THEME: Materialism and social injustice will bring judgment

OVERVIEW:

Amos was just a poor shepherd from a small town in the south. He loved God and could be trusted. God knew that He could use Amos because of his obedience, not because of his skills. That's such a common choice by God throughout the entire Bible. He always uses the least qualified and through that, He is able to show His power and receive the glory.

Amos starts off by directing the judgment towards all of the Gentile enemies in order to get Israel on his side, and then he drops the bomb by giving them their own judgment. And it wasn't pretty. But Amos was a strong man of prayer. He was confident in his relationship with the Father and knew that He cared about what Amos had to say. So, when Amos receives terrible visions of judgment coming upon God's people, he pleads on behalf of them and God ends up showing them mercy by not following through. The God from back then is the same God whom we serve today. The Father is more than willing to change His plans if we provide Him with a good reason to do so.

JOURNAL:

Name a few ordinary people in modern culture that God has used to do great things:

Sharing testimonies of answered prayer builds up faith within us. So, what are a few examples of answered prayer in your life?

ISAIAH OVERVIEW
AUTHOR: The prophet Isaiah
DATE: 700-680 BC
AUDIENCE: The southern kingdom
THEME: Judgment and salvation

OVERVIEW:

Isaiah is the first of the "Major Prophet" books of the Old Testament. He is known as the "Messianic Prophet" because of how often he prophecies of Jesus' arrival.

Old Testament prophecy is almost always the same, and if you read through all of the prophetic books you will notice that there are a lot of promises for future judgment and eventual restoration. The prophetic books can seem very repetitive, but if you truly dive in, you'll see the importance in every one of them.

Not only does the book of Isaiah promise restoration for the nation of Israel, but it also promises that the Messiah will arise from the House of David. With that said, the New Testament quotes from Isaiah more than any other prophet because he had so much to say about the coming King, Jesus.

JOURNAL:

Using your New Testament understanding of the Messiah, read Isaiah 53, and take the rest of this page to explain to a Jewish person why Jesus is their Messiah after all. It's not an easy task, but it's important to be able to do. Have fun with it!

MICAH OVERVIEW

AUTHOR: The prophet Micah

DATE: 700-686 BC

AUDIENCE: Political and religious leaders of
Judah

THEME: Judgment against social injustice

OVERVIEW:

The prophets Isaiah and Micah were contemporaries of their time. Many people believe that Micah was a disciple of Isaiah, calling his book the "Little Isaiah". Both prophets were speaking into the same situation. Both ended up being ignored by the masses.

Unlike Isaiah, Micah came from a small town where he knew the social injustice of the wealthy all too well. These were his people. His life. So, you can feel the emotion in his words as he speaks. Micah was going to do everything in his power to stop the injustice from spreading. And instead of attacking them with anger, he wept and showed them what true love was. That's a very "new testament way" of approaching injustice. Micah was after their hearts, not their minds.

JOURNAL:

Are you involved in any groups against social injustice? Which category are you most passionate about?

How does Jesus deal with social injustice? With Jesus as an example, what can we do on behalf of those that are hurting?

NAHUM OVERVIEW
AUTHOR: The prophet Nahum
DATE: 663-612 BC
AUDIENCE: Nineveh and Judah
THEME: The fall of Nineveh

OVERVIEW:

Nahum seems like a real patriotic fellow, similar to Jonah 150 years before him. They both preached judgment towards Nineveh, and they both had different outcomes. Nahum is a book of destruction. There is no turning back with his prophecy. Judgment was going to come whether they repented or not.

At this time, the best place to be was in Judah because God promised that He would wipe out their enemies and protect them in the end. God wanted to comfort them even when there was a threat of exile looming on the horizon.

Jumping back to Nineveh, Nahum shows that they are far past redemption. God knew that they wouldn't change again, no matter what He did for them. Yes, God forgives sin, but if you remain in your sin, He will turn against you. Being a new creation means that you are moving from glory to glory. You are no longer a sinner. You are now a saint. Remaining in sin contradicts your entire nature. After being saved, you literally have to choose to separate yourself from God and continue to sin. He doesn't want that. And you shouldn't either.

JOURNAL:

What do you think it means to be moving from glory to glory?

Do you remember what it means to be a new creation? How does that change the way you think about yourself?

ZEPHANIAH OVERVIEW

AUTHOR: The prophet Zephaniah

DATE: 640-621 BC

AUDIENCE: The southern kingdom

THEME: Seek righteousness before the Day of the Lord

OVERVIEW:

The book of Zephaniah is a short prophecy that warned the southern kingdom of Judah about the coming "Day of the Lord", and that set the tone for the rest of the book. Israel was already taken into exile, so they are the last remaining group that has a chance of being free from judgment if they turned from their sins. Although that may be easier said than done.

Zephaniah urges them to join together as one, in order that they all repent and possibly be saved as a nation. He also shares about how God will judge the other nations who are the enemies of Israel. The Lord promises to diminish them for their pride and taunting because He always fights on behalf of His people. No matter what judgment the Lord may have put His people through, He always had the upper hand and protected them in the end. That's why the Jewish people have never been wiped out, no matter how much persecution they have gone through.

JOURNAL:

Have you ever witnessed God fight on your behalf? What happened?

What do you know about the nation of Israel today? Do you believe that God still protects His people?

SUNDAY.
SUNDAY.
SUNDAY.
SUNDAY.
SUNDAY.

BEST
DAY
OF THE
WEEK

JEREMIAH OVERVIEW

AUTHOR: The priest-prophet Jeremiah

DATE: 626-580 BC

AUDIENCE: The southern kingdom

THEME: The fall of Jerusalem and the reason for their exile

OVERVIEW:

Jeremiah was known as "the weeping prophet" because he really put his heart into his prophecies. His words hit you on the inside and you get to know his personality much better than the other prophets.

The majority of the book is about destruction and judgment that was to come to Judah and the surrounding nations for remaining unrepentant. Same story; different prophet.

One thing that makes Jeremiah stand out is that he writes in poetry for the entire book. It shows that the Father is communicating His heart towards the audience instead of His mind, like we see when a writer uses what is called "prose". Poetry is deeper and shares the feelings of the Father. Prose is more effective to get the point across. So, Jeremiah shared a lot about the heart of the Father and the importance of getting your heart right with God instead of being religious with your actions.

JOURNAL:

Do you ever write your thoughts in a journal? If so, do you write in poetry or prose?

What do you think it means to communicate the heart of the Father?

LAMENTATIONS OVERVIEW

AUTHOR: Unknown, but probably Jeremiah

DATE: 586-580 BC

AUDIENCE: Jews in exile

THEME: Sorrow over Jerusalem and the compassion of God

OVERVIEW:

Most scholars believe that Lamentations was also written by Jeremiah, which makes a lot of sense being that he was called "the weeping prophet". Lamentations is proof of that.

After multiple prophecies of Jerusalem's future destruction, their time was finally coming to pass because they had failed to repent as Jeremiah had pleaded. Jerusalem was destroyed before their eyes, and the people were taken away to exile. It was a horrific time to be alive. And Jeremiah wept. It's one of the saddest books you could ever read.

But there was hope! Jeremiah realized that through God's mercy He chose to keep a group alive. He was seeing the good inside of the bad and found something to be thankful for even when the situation looked terrible. Jeremiah took that revelation and prayed into it that God would one day be so merciful that the nation of Israel would be restored. And history shows us that the Lord answered it!

JOURNAL:

With that said, spend a few minutes listening to the song "Mercy" by Amanda Cook. Then spend the rest of the page journaling what you sense the Father saying to you through that song and what His views on judgment / mercy are.

HABABKKUK OVERVIEW

AUTHOR: The prophet Habakkuk

DATE: 609-605 BC

AUDIENCE: Religious and political people
                   of Judah

THEME: The righteous will live by faith

OVERVIEW:

Habakkuk was a man who questioned everything. He wrestled with God until he received an answer that was fitting for his narrow perspective. But Habakkuk wasn't God, so some things would never fully make sense. Same with today, we can wrestle as much as we want, but in the end, some things will remain a mystery.

In this book, Habakkuk is asking very basic questions that contradict his view of the Father's heart. I think it's a good idea to question things you don't understand in order to align your heart with His. So many times, we place God in a box that fits our doctrine properly but contradicts some of Scripture. That's never a good spot to be in. Habakkuk expected God to act a certain way, and when He didn't, that's when the questions began to fly.

JOURNAL:

What are some of the "big" questions in life that you tend to wrestle with?

Habakkuk spent a lot of time praying and waiting, what prayers are you waiting for God to respond about?

_____
_____
_____
_____
_____
_____
_____
_____
_____
_____
_____
_____
_____
_____
_____
_____
_____
_____

EZEKIEL OVERVIEW

AUTHOR: The priest-prophet Ezekiel

DATE: 593-571 BC

AUDIENCE: The exiles in Babylon

THEME: God's sovereignty over all people and His glory

DAY SEVENTY SEVEN

OVERVIEW:

The book of Ezekiel is a book of hope. Ezekiel was one of the only guys in exile that God shared His plan of redemption with. Ezekiel could either share it or keep his insight to himself. He chose to share it because it provided hope to all of the Israelites since they just had their entire lives stripped from them. He provided hope in order to show them that life was actually worth living.

Even though the prophecies from Ezekiel contain a whole lot of prophetic destruction at the beginning, through it all, the Lord promises a future restoration for the people of Israel. The restoration was not a reward for their good behavior or anything that they could physically do, because when it came down to it, they always ended up failing. The restoration was completely for God's sake so that He would be represented accurately. This book is full of vivid imagery and talks about some stuff that will still happen in the future.

JOURNAL:

Is it easy for you to find the good in bad situations?

What is the most hopeless area of your life right now? Write down two positives that you can find in that situation.

DANIEL OVERVIEW

AUTHOR: The prophet Daniel

DATE: 540-530 BC

AUDIENCE: The exiles in Babylon

THEME: The kingdom of God will reign supreme for eternity

OVERVIEW:

The book of Daniel is full of stories and prophecies, both natural and supernatural. In the beginning of the book we see stories like the popular one of Daniel in the Lion's den, which I'm sure many of you remember as a child. Later on in the book, there are many prophecies that have been fulfilled already and many that are still to come. Daniel is known as the "Revelation of the Old Testament" because of its focus on the end times. Some revelations are easy to understand, and some are a little harder and unclear.

Over time, Daniel is given a backstage pass to Babylonian royalty and ends up being one of the leading actors because of his relationship with King Nebuchadnezzar. Not only is this Daniel's story, but it also shows how God was protecting His people, even during their punishment in exile.

JOURNAL:

How has God shown you favor among unbelievers?

In what areas of your life have you dealt with trials and saw that God was faithful in helping you through? Give an example.

EZRA OVERVIEW

AUTHOR: The priest Ezra

DATE: Sometime after 433 BC

AUDIENCE: The exiles in Babylon

THEME: God's sovereignty over all people and His glory

OVERVIEW:

The book of Ezra records what happens directly following the nation of Israel's 70 years in Babylon, and how easily they went right back into sin.

The new world power at the time, Persia, took over Babylon under the leadership of a man named Cyrus. In 538 BC he made a decree that allowed all of the Jews to go back to Jerusalem and he even gave the Jewish remnant all of the materials necessary for rebuilding their temple.

The process took 23 years to build the Second Temple, but it wasn't nearly as magnificent as Solomon's Temple. That bummed some of the people out because Cyrus had provided enough materials for it to be great, but the remnant didn't take advantage of their gifts.

By the time Ezra was sent to Jerusalem, the temple had already been built for almost 60 years and they were in rough shape. So, Ezra was on a mission to restore their faith. And he did.

JOURNAL:

What do you think was going through the Jewish people's minds when they were allowed to go back to Jerusalem?

Why do you think they failed to take advantage of their gifts?

NEHEMIAH OVERVIEW

AUTHOR: The priest Ezra

DATE: Sometime after 433 BC

AUDIENCE: Jews returning from Babylon

THEME: Restoring the city and the people

OVERVIEW:

The books of Ezra and Nehemiah were originally written together by Ezra himself. In the book of Ezra, we see Ezra coming in to restore the Jewish people's faith. In the book of Nehemiah, we see Nehemiah coming in to restore their city. He was the new governor in town and the people were ready to listen. First things first were to build a wall around the city for protection and to give the people roles that fit their skillset.

Once the wall was built, Ezra enters the scene again. While Nehemiah was the champion of social and political influence, Ezra brought them home from a spiritual perspective. When Ezra spoke, everyone listened. The people actually begged for more. This was a defining moment for the people of Israel and the future nation as a whole. It was a fresh start. New. Improved. Doing things differently this time around.

JOURNAL:

Has anything happened in your life that caused you to change from your old ways? If so, did you change cold turkey or was it a gradual process?

Do any pastors that you listen to leave you begging for more? Who? What is it about them that makes you want to keep listening?

ESTHER OVERVIEW

AUTHOR: Unknown

DATE: Around 460 BC

AUDIENCE: The Israelites under
Persian control

THEME: Saving God's people

OVERVIEW:

The book of Esther is an amazing story of how God protected His people from extinction yet again. We're dealing with the Jews that chose not to return to Jerusalem from exile because of either social or work-related reasons. And God still chose to protect them.

It's a story of a Jewish woman named Esther, who became the queen of Persia to King Ahasuerus without him knowing she was Jewish. There was a man named Haman that worked for the king who hated the Jews with all of his heart. His plan was to kill them all. Esther's relative, Mordecai, heard of Haman's plan and begged her to do something about it. After building up enough courage, Esther threw two different feasts for the king and on the final day she pleaded for him to save the Jewish people. King Ahasuerus granted her request and ended up saving their entire people group.

JOURNAL:

Give at least one historical example of an attempt to wipe out the Jewish race:

How should the Church respond to anti-Semitism (hatred towards Jews)?

HAGGAI OVERVIEW

AUTHOR: The prophet Haggai

DATE: 520 BC

AUDIENCE: The returning remnant

THEME: Finish rebuilding the temple

OVERVIEW:

Whereas most Old Testament prophets prophesied over a large span of time, Haggai had four short messages that he shared in under five months. And his tone was also different. Haggai wasn't preaching judgment like the others, he was encouraging them to keep going with the temple. He knew they weren't living up to their capacity, so he chose to speak words of encouragement regarding their talents.

Haggai just wanted to share how pleased the Father would be once the building itself was complete. The Lord didn't necessarily even care what the building looked like or how it was decorated, He just wanted it to EXIST so that He could live among them again. It's the ability to live together and the obedience of the people that He cares the most about.

And after Haggai got done encouraging them, the people turned from their ways and kept building the temple. He also delivered a message to the priests because they were the ones that knew the Law best. He made it clear that just because they were touching / working on the temple it didn't make them holy. The Lord cares about the heart and that's it.

JOURNAL:

Has someone ever spoken a word of encouragement to you that motivated you to keep going? What was it?

Have you ever stepped out in faith? How did God provide for your needs?

ZECHARIAH OVERVIEW

AUTHOR: The priest-prophet Zechariah

DATE: 518 and 480 BC

AUDIENCE: The returning remnant

THEME: The current temple and the future temple

OVERVIEW:

Zechariah is one of the most messianic books in the entire Old Testament, with thirty total messianic prophecies. It is jam-packed with prophetic visions of the immediate and distant future. Visions in the Bible are not necessarily the easiest to things to understand. And in some cases, the interpretation is in the eye of the beholder, while other times they are obvious. Since we are looking at Zechariah's visions from the future, we can pick out what has already happened and what still needs to take place.

In Zechariah we see him prophesying that Jesus would ride in on a donkey.

He would be betrayed for 30 pieces of silver.

His body would be pierced.

He would be the Cornerstone and the Branch.

Israel would be scattered as a result of his death.

And the list goes on. It blows my mind how spot-on it is.

JOURNAL:

Has the Lord ever spoken to you through visions or dreams? If so, when? Have you seen them fulfilled?

What are your thoughts on all of these Old Testament prophecies being fulfilled through Jesus? Wild, right?

MALACHI OVERVIEW

AUTHOR: The prophet Malachi

DATE: 430-420 BC

AUDIENCE: The remnant of Israel

THEME: Judgment will come unless they return to the Lord

OVERVIEW:

At the time that Malachi was writing this prophecy, Jerusalem was in rough shape. The Israelites were doing alright by their own standards, but the main city was far from their central focus. They became selfish. Content. Satisfied. A good relationship with God was the last thing that they were focused on because they felt God had left. And the priests didn't take it seriously, so why should the citizens?

The Lord directs His attention to the wickedness of the priests right off the bat and calls them out for their polluted offerings. All that they offered was in vain, so the Lord wouldn't accept it as sincere. He demands worship. Awe. Only when people treat Him as He deserves to be treated will the offerings be accepted the way that they want them to be accepted…as purification and blessing. The main problem that the Israelites were dealing with is that they were messing with God's name… who He is. That's a big no-no. He has a reputation to hold on to and anything or anyone that tries to defame Him is not taken lightly.

As you probably know, Malachi is the last book of the Old Testament. The last three verses are centered around two of the greatest men that the Israelites knew: Moses and Elijah. It's God's last appeal to Israel before 400 years of silence. He told them to get back to the ways of Moses, and God would give them another chance. And that was the last thing they heard from Him for a very long time.

JOURNAL:

What promises has God given you that have yet to be fulfilled? Is there anything that you can do to speed up the process? Do you need to step out in obedience?

Why do you think God went silent for 400 years after this?

NO OTHER NAME

———

JESUS
JESUS
JESUS

THE FULFILLMENT

Over the next five days, we will be digging into the Gospel of Matthew. I think it's important to study this last because it shows the fulfillment of the Old Testament through Jesus.

READ: Matthew 1-7

AUTHOR: Matthew, a disciple and former tax collector

DATE: AD 50-55

AUDIENCE: The Jews

THEME: Jesus is the Jewish Messiah

DAY EIGHTY FOUR

OVERVIEW:

The Gospel of Matthew is the first book in the New Testament, which is important because Matthew is a Jew writing to the Jews and he shows them that their Messiah has arrived. It's a phenomenal book of fulfillment.

Since we just spent so much time looking at the Old Testament books, one thing to remember is to put yourself in the shoes of the original reader so that you can better understand what is being taught. In this case, Matthew uses far more Old Testament quotes than the other Gospel writers and doesn't feel obligated to explain the Jewish lifestyle. The audience would have understood all of it.

JOURNAL:

How well do you understand Jesus being the fulfillment of the Jewish Messiah? Do you feel like you need more teaching on it or are you good?

What is the most important thing that God taught you through today's reading?

How can you apply that to your life?

READ: Matthew 8-13

AUTHOR: Matthew, a disciple and former
tax collector

DATE: AD 50-55

AUDIENCE: The Jews

THEME: Jesus is the Jewish Messiah

DAY EIGHTY FIVE

JOURNAL:

As we see in Chapter 13, Jesus loved
speaking in parables to his audiences.
Why does Jesus speak in parables?
(Matthew 13:13-17)

What is the most important thing that
God taught you through today's reading?

How can you apply that to your life?

READ: Matthew 14-18

AUTHOR: Matthew, a disciple and former
tax collector

DATE: AD 50-55

AUDIENCE: The Jews

THEME: Jesus is the Jewish Messiah

DAY EIGHTY SIX

JOURNAL:

There were a lot of miraculous stories
highlighted today. Which one do you find
is the most interesting? Why?

What is the most important thing that
God taught you through today's reading?

How can you apply that to your life?

READ: Matthew 19-25

AUTHOR: Matthew, a disciple and former tax collector

DATE: AD 50-55

AUDIENCE: The Jews

THEME: Jesus is the Jewish Messiah

DAY EIGHTY SEVEN

JOURNAL:

What is the main focus of each of Jesus' five sermons?

1. (Matthew 5-7)

2. (Matthew 10)

3. (Matthew 13)

4. (Matthew 18)

5. (Matthew 23-25)

How do they relate with each other?

READ: Matthew 26-28

AUTHOR: Matthew, a disciple and former tax collector

DATE: AD 50-55

AUDIENCE: The Jews

THEME: Jesus is the Jewish Messiah

DAY EIGHTY EIGHT

JOURNAL:

The last words of Jesus that Matthew records, are, "All authority in heaven and on earth has been given to me. Go therefore and make disciples of all nations, baptizing them in the name of the Father and of the Son and of the Holy Spirit, teaching them to observe all that I have commanded you. And behold, I am with you always, to the end of the age" (28:18b-20 ESV). That statement is what is known as the Great Commission.

In what ways are you fulfilling the Great Commission? How can you improve?

What is the most important thing that God taught you through today's reading?

How can you apply that to your life?

DAY EIGHTY NINE

JOURNAL:

Before we say our "goodbyes" there is one final thing that I would like you to do - use the next page to explain the Gospel message in an easy-to-understand way that you can use in the future for evangelism.

As we just saw yesterday, Matthew 28:19 says, "Go therefore and make disciples of all nations, baptizing them in the name of the Father and of the Son and of the Holy Spirit" (ESV). Now that you know the Word so well, go and share it! Make disciples! Spread the LOVE of our Father!

DAY NINETY

JOURNAL:

WOW! You just completed The Bible Study Youth Edition! Amazing!

Take a moment to reflect on the past 90 days and how God transformed your heart throughout the process.

Where are you at on your faith journey now?

What was the most important thing that God taught you through this process?

How do you plan on continuing to study the Bible?

ABOUT THE AUTHOR

THE AUTHOR

Zach Windahl is an entrepreneur who loves helping others realize their identity and encouraging them to chase their dreams. Zach grew up a Christian, but in 2014 he went on a journey to Australia in search of the God of the Bible. He needed his stagnant faith to become real. God showed up and completely transformed Zach's life. He splits his time between Minneapolis, Minnesota and south Florida.

THE
BIBLE
IS
GOOD
FOR
YOU